£12.95

D1326542

The
Young Freud

The Young Freud

The Origins of Psychoanalysis in
Late Nineteenth-Century Viennese Culture

BILLA ZANUSO

Basil Blackwell

English translation © Basil Blackwell Ltd 1986

Originally published in Italian as *La Nascita della Psicoanalisi: Freud nella cultura della Vienna fine secolo* copyright © 1982 by Bompiani

First published in English 1986

Basil Blackwell Ltd
108 Cowley Road, Oxford OX4 1JF, UK

Basil Blackwell Inc.
432 Park Avenue South, Suite 1503,
New York, NY 10016, USA

British Library Cataloguing in Publication Data

Zanuso, Billa
The young Freud: the origins of
psychoanalysis in late nineteenth-century
Viennese culture.
1. Freud, Sigmund   2. Psychoanalysis
I. Title   II. Nascita della psicoanalisi.
English
150.19'52   BF173.F85

ISBN 0-631-13749-1

Library of Congress Cataloging in Publication Data

Zanuso, Billa.
    The young Freud.

    Translation of: La nascita della psicoanalisi.
    Bibliography: p.
    Includes index.
    1. Psychoanalysis–Austria–Vienna–History–19th
century.   2. Freud, Sigmund, 1856–1939.   3. Vienna
(Austria)–History–19th century.   I. Title.
BF175.Z3313   1986   150.19'52   86-13621
ISBN 0-631-13749-1

Printed in the USA

Contents

Acknowledgements

The publishers wish to acknowledge the work of the translator in the preparation of the English edition of this book, while respecting her preference for anonymity. The publishers wish further to thank the author, Polly Buston and Dr Christopher Badcock for their invaluable help, the latter especially for his work in establishing the correct English text of quotations from Freud.

Part I

The Age of Freud

1

Vienna, the Bourgeois City

The Freud scandal

'Psycho-analysis brings forward so much that is new, and among it so much that contradicts traditional opinions and wounds deep-rooted feelings, that it is bound at first to provoke denial.' So Freud warns in his preface to the Hebrew edition of *Introductory Lectures on Psycho-Analysis* (standard edn, vol. XV, p. 11).[1] This series of lectures outlining his theory of psychoanalysis was originally delivered to an audience of doctors and laymen in Vienna between 1916 and 1917. By the time of this preface, published in 1930, the importance of psychoanalysis had long been recognized in international scientific circles. Yet Freud admits that the new perspectives opened up by this science can, and even should, produce an adverse reaction. This view is easier to understand when one considers the period in which Freud published his works and takes into consideration the traditional and deep-rooted feelings Freud offended with his theory.

Let us go back to Habsburg Vienna in the second half of the nineteenth century. Vienna, where Freud lived and worked, was the capital of the Austro-Hungarian Empire. The major

[1] See also *Complete Introductory Lectures on Psycho-Analysis* (London, 1971).

influence in Europe at that time was Germany, which under Bismarck had become a threatening military power while enjoying at the same time extraordinary industrial and commercial growth. Second in importance, but only just, was France, which was less militarized and had a less developed industry, but none the less challenged Germany's scientific, artistic and commercial supremacy. Paris was then the great cultural centre of Europe, where painting, music and literature flourished in an atmosphere conducive to intellectual, artistic and personal freedom. Unlike Germany and France, the Austro-Hungarian Empire was not one nation, but a mosaic of different peoples — Czechs, Italians, Serbians, Croats, Slavs, Hungarians, Poles and Austrians. Over all of these reigned the Emperor Franz-Josef, who had come to power in 1848 at a critical point in the fortunes of the Habsburg dynasty, for a mood of revolution had threatened to undermine the oppressive rule of the previous Emperor, Franz I, and of his henchman, Metternich.

'My kingdom is a worm-eaten house', observed Franz I bitterly, to justify his lack of flexibility. 'Take away part of it, and the rest might collapse.' When Franz-Josef succeeded, he found himself in a difficult situation. The vast composite Empire was threatened from without by the expansionist ambitions of Germany and France, and from within by its subject states whose nationalistic claims perpetually threatened its stability. Franz-Josef, like his predecessor, Franz I, strove to maintain the status quo. In his book on the Habsburg myth in modern Austrian literature, Claudio Magris points out that during his 68-year reign even Franz-Josef's apparently progressive political moves were really conservative in purpose. The Emperor's motto was Law and Order, which he achieved by means of bureaucracy and the army. The vision which was intended to give this fundamentally static programme the semblance of a sacred long-term mission was one of many peoples united under the sovereign sway of the divinely appointed Habsburg Father, in the name of peace, harmony and prosperity. As capital of the Empire, Vienna had to project this ambitious image with a show of magnificence. In 1857, a year after Freud's birth, the ancient walls, which could no longer contain a rapidly increasing population, were pulled down; the city was encircled by a broad avenue, the Ringstrasse, flanked by buildings that would house the newly emerging industrial and commercial middle class which had replaced the now impotent aristocracy. More buildings were erected: a university, museums, scientific institutes, cultural centres, libraries and art schools testified to the cultural revolution in which the middle classes played the leading part. During the second half of the nineteenth century the University of Vienna was renowned throughout Europe for its high standards of research and teaching, especially in the field of medicine. New theatres, including the Opera House, were also built, as were a number of concert halls and musical academies, where performers and public alike were drawn from the cultured middle classes, giving the Vienna of the day its particular tone.

It was a hybrid culture, showing signs of the aristocrat's refined aestheticism, the scientist's impartial search for truth and the moral rectitude and sense of tradition of the emergent managerial class. It was this image of man, the product of this moral tradition and this culture, that Freud's discoveries most vigorously attacked.

We are not concerned here with that section of Viennese society which expressed in art, drama and literature the anxieties, ideas and discoveries of a class which, as the Empire itself crumbled, nurtured an incredibly rich cultural movement. On the contrary, our interest lies in that mass of people 'possessed with an indestructible concept of life' who, unaffected by the atmosphere of febrile excitement that permeated the 'thin, inconsistent strata of the intelligentsia, continued to exist, to act and to evolve according to a traditional human pattern — who were that is, traditionally bourgeois' (Musil, *The Man Without Qualities*).

The good citizen

In this respect Viennese society was no different from other contemporary Western societies, the archetype being Victorian England where, conscious of representing his age, country and class, a man was expected to behave in a certain way and exhibit certain qualities, these having been formed by his education within his family, his school and the society in which he lived. These qualities were perseverance, a sense of duty, obedience to moral and civil laws and a respect for the rights of others; but he should also show initiative, be hard working and be able to seize any opportunities life might offer in order to improve his position through honest and responsible effort. He should appreciate honestly earned and well-managed wealth, but live frugally in order to fund other ventures. Here was the perfect model for those classes which saw industrial expansion as an excellent opportunity for consolidating their own positions.

In *The Protestant Ethic and the Spirit of Capitalism* Max Weber observes:

> When the limitation of consumption is combined with this release of acquisitive activity, the inevitable practical result is obvious: accumulation of capital . . .
> What the great religious epoch of the seventeenth century bequeathed to its utilitarian successor was, however, above all an amazingly good, we may even say a pharisaically good, conscience in the acquisition of money so long as it took place legally . . .
> A specifically bourgeois economic ethic had grown up. With the consciousness of standing in the fullness of God's grace and being visibly blessed by Him, the bourgeois business

man, as long as he remained within the bounds of formal correctness, as long as his moral conduct was spotless and the use to which he put his wealth was not objectionable, could follow his pecuniary interests as he would and feel that he was fulfilling a duty in doing so. The power of religious asceticism provided him in addition with sober, conscientious and unusually industrious workmen, who clung to their purpose as to a life purpose willed by God.

Finally, it gave him the comforting assurance that the unequal distribution of the goods of this world was a special dispensation of Divine Providence, which in these differences, as in particular grace, pursued secret ends unknown to men. (pp. 176—7)

Edifying literature

During the latter half of the nineteenth century popular edifying works that presented this model in a more or less alluring light were published throughout Europe for the benefit of young people and 'the masses', these latter being considered equally immature and in need of guidance. These books were bought by schools and parents, and they were recommended reading for adolescents, but they were particularly meant to be read aloud by parents and teachers so that the principles they expounded might be communicated 'live', as it were.

The Scot Samuel Smiles wrote books in the genre which enjoyed enormous success in England, but they were also translated into most European languages, and into Indian and Japanese. It is evident therefore that the ethics peculiar to that time were the ethics of a class: they were not restricted by national frontiers, and were intended to provide a working model for the managerial class on whose success the ascendancy of Western societies depended.

The titles of Smiles's books speak for themselves: *Self-Help*

(1850) praises personal initiative in the form of hard work and study; *Character* (1872) praises tenacity and perseverance, whereby a man may acquire the qualities which ennoble those not born titled and wealthy; *Duty* (1880) praises the self-educated man who, through strict self-discipline, becomes his own master and wins public acclaim.

Michele Lessona's *Volere e potere* (*To Will Is To Achieve*, 1928) is written in similar vein ('since in Italy the time for revolutions is over, and our future depends entirely on intelligent hard work'). It is a collection of anecdotes, biographies and portraits of his well-known and less well-known compatriots aimed at providing an example to Italian youth. The theme of the book is that if you work hard and are thrifty you will earn the approbation of the powers that be, and if you know how to take advantage of this you too may become rich and powerful, will enjoy the respect of your neighbour and God's blessing and will serve your country well. Then comes the conclusion:

> contempt for wealth is a terrible ill, a hereditary disease, as it were, since we have inherited it from aristocrats ... By contrast, the benefits of honestly pursued and honestly earned wealth are immense. Satisfaction is to be gained from labouring in pursuit of it, the mind is given something to aim at, to consider from every angle — looking for flaws, correcting and improving on original ideas, coaxing something into being, dealing with difficulties and hardship, sometimes having to start again from scratch, to abandon one attempt and make another; then after all the set-backs and disappointments comes renewed hope, success, then further reversals followed by further triumphs, and the final achievement that makes up for everything and brings with it the energy and courage to undertake something new and worthwhile.
>
> In the meantime, people who hitherto never spared you a thought, and who perhaps even laughed at you, begin to make way for you, to eye you benevolently, to show signs of

respect; you will be surrounded by flattery; but since you
have learned from experience to recognize its blandishments
you keep your distance and are not its dupe.

Life does not become easier, on the contrary, new and
unforeseen mishaps occur; but you know how to win through,
you sprint off again; you are motivated by thoughts of a
bright future and a good education for your children, establishing your own good name, and the pleasures of the
improving conversations you will have with them, all of
which help you to overcome the inevitable trials of life; and
there is also the joy of being able to put your honourably
acquired wealth to a more public use, by helping those who
deserve help and by supporting the nation's charities that are
useful and decent. (Translator's version)

The image of man which emerges from these texts is
extremely encouraging, or, one might say, edifying. If a man
is of a willing disposition, no obstacle will stand in the way of
his progress. He will be in control of his material and spiritual
world, since both respect the will to do what is right. This is
not difficult to achieve since all that is required is obedience
from the start to the moral code inherent in a healthy family
upbringing. According to Smiles, the civilization of a nation
depends on the character of its individuals, and it is on these
that the well-being of a society rests.

We find an exact replica of this ideal man or citizen in the
work of the Austrian writer Adalbert Stifter. He too sees the
strength of the state as being dependent on the moral fibre or
self-discipline of its inhabitants. As Carl Schorske points out
in *'Fin de Siècle' Vienna: Politics and Culture*, Stifter saw the
subjection and control of the passions as an integral and
indispensable aspect of both individual and state freedom:
'genuine freedom demands the most self-control, the con-
straint of one's desires . . . The foremost and only enemies of
freedom therefore are all those people who are possessed by
powerful desires and urges, which they wish to gratify by any

means' (p. 281). In his story *Der Nachsommer* (*Indian Summer*) Stifter gives a fictional example of what he means by *Bildung* or that inner strength which is conducive to true freedom: 'Whoever is morally free can be politically free and always is so; not all the powers of the earth can make the others free. There is but one power which can do so: *Bildung*' (p. 282).

The author deals with Heinrich's journey throughout life, but of particular interest is the description of his childhood which recreates that atmosphere of benevolent paternalism based on a strict hierarchy, that painful apprenticeship in obedience and duty and that tireless diligence which we have already come across in the edifying propaganda mentioned above. Schorske comments here:

> In this household [Heinrich's] old-style commercial enterprise and an upright family life are felicitously united under the sober justice of the father-master . . . Heinrich Drendorf begins his story with the lapidary sentence 'My father was a merchant.' Domicile and shop were under the same roof. The employees ate at the master's table as members of an enlarged family. The ethic of fatherhood governed the elder Drendorf's behaviour as entrepreneur. The obverse was equally true: Drendorf's early capitalist ethic informed his exercise of paternal authority. He managed his family and his household, one might say, like a business in an era when probity, thrift, simplicity, and strict personal accountability were the principal economic virtues. Every person had his appointed duties in the household. Time and space were precisely subdivided and organized in such a fashion that every segment fulfilled a specified function. Heinrich's mother, a warm and good-natured soul who would have allowed her children a more spontaneous life, enforced 'out of fear of Father' the appointed tasks laid down by the master of the household. The well-ordered environment was the key to the well-ordered soul, and together they composed the well-ordered world. (Ibid., pp. 284—5)

If this was indeed the conventional image of man, Freud's theories must have caused a considerable scandal among his contemporaries. Freud's research began as a therapeutic method of dealing with psychoneuroses and was therefore mainly the concern of those whose specific function was to cure similar affections; but research in this field revealed certain aspects of psychic activity hitherto ignored or neglected, and it gradually became a general psychology involving the study of both pathological and normal behaviour. An image of man began to emerge from Freud's inquiries that was in total contrast to the conventional one. It particularly shocked the methodical, conservative middle classes who believed (and were determined to believe) that they were the foundations upon which the Habsburg Empire's vast realm was built and that the structure of their private family life was a replica in miniature of the great imperial structure personified by the paternal and immutable figure of Franz-Josef.

Man is not master in his own house

What was becoming apparent through Freudian research was that that part of an individual which acts in accordance with existing conventions, which manages to bridle emotions and passions in obedience to an accepted authority and is able to achieve whatever it sets out to do, is only a fraction of the human personality, that fraction which is most easily seen. Beneath and beyond this part lies a whole range of psychological phenomena, inaccessible to the conscious mind, interacting with it and unknown to it, determining its behaviour.

Thus man, far from being master of the world and of exterior events, is not even master in his own house. Freud was well aware of the scandalous nature of such an assertion.

But in thus emphasizing the unconscious in mental life we have conjured up the most evil spirits of criticism against psycho-analysis. Do not be surprised at this, and do not suppose that the resistance to us rests only on the understandable difficulty of the unconscious or the relative inaccessibility of the experiences which provide evidence of it. Its source, I think, lies deeper. In the course of centuries the *naïve* self-love of men has had to submit to two major blows at the hands of science. The first was when they learnt that our earth was not the centre of the universe but only a tiny fragment of a cosmic system of scarcely imaginable vastness. This is associated in our minds with the name of Copernicus, though something similar had already been asserted by Alexandrian science. The second blow fell when biological research destroyed man's supposedly privileged place in creation and proved his descent from the animal kingdom and his ineradicable animal nature. This revaluation has been accomplished in our own days by Darwin, Wallace and their predecessors, though not without the most violent contemporary opposition. But human megalomania will have suffered its third and most wounding blow from the psychological research of the present time which seeks to prove to the ego that it is not even master in its own house, but must content itself with scanty information of what is going on unconsciously in its mind. We psychoanalysts were not the first and not the only ones to utter this call to introspection; but it seems to be our fate to give it its most forcible expression and to support it with empirical material which affects every individual. Hence arises the general revolt against our science, the disregard of all considerations of academic civility and the releasing of the opposition from every restraint of impartial logic. (*Introductory Lectures on Psycho-Analysis*, standard edn, vol. XVI, pp. 284—5)

Dual personality

The idea that the personality had a deeper layer over which we have no control was not something Freud himself had discovered. Nor was this notion considered particularly surprising or scandalous. The possibility had already been suggested, and even put to the test, to a certain extent. As we shall see, famous physicians specializing in nervous illnesses, particularly hysteria, had acknowledged the scientific value of hypnosis, that is, of a therapeutic method whereby an artificial sleep is induced during which memories, emotions and impulses surface that the patient when awake cannot recall; there were even some stage hypnotists who would make spectators perform a series of actions after putting them into a state of trance. Several novels of the period features heroes whose 'doubles' surfaced under the influence of mysterious drugs or of evil or hypnotic powers of one sort or another.

The theme of the double runs through nineteenth-century literature from the tales of E. T. A. Hoffmann in the first years of the century — notably in *The Devil's Elixirs* (1813—16) — to Poe's *Tales* (1839—46), while a number of works, some popular then but now forgotten, others of lasting literary merit, interpreted this theme in various ways. Ellenberger's *The Discovery of the Unconscious* gives a brilliant account of the genre and is well worth reading. I shall therefore restrict myself to a few words on the most important works.

One of Dostoevsky's earliest novels, *The Double* (1846), tells of the painful experiences of the clerk Goljadkin, initially a quiet, irreproachable character, who gradually deteriorates into madness and the madhouse. In this book psychotic disturbances are seen as 'another self' which the hero holds responsible for his strange behaviour. This other self is identified as the dreaded persecutor who first insinuates himself in the guise of a humble and needy companion, and then becomes invasive and hostile until he finally deprives the protagonist of all his possessions and friends and drives him to his ruin.

Another type of dual personality is depicted in *The Picture of Dorian Grey* by Oscar Wilde, still widely read today. Here the duality occurs between a portrait of Dorian painted in the immaculate bloom of youth and the hero himself destined as are all men to age and decay. Through the supernatural fulfilment of a wish it is the portrait which shows all the scars of the hero's depraved existence, while he himself still radiates youth and beauty. But the trick cannot last, and as Dorian contemplates the evidence of his moral decadence as depicted in the features of the portrait, he is so overcome with anguish that he stabs the canvas; whereupon he falls dead, and assumes in death the ravaged corrupt appearance which is his by rights. The portrait alone remains to immortalize his lost youth and beauty. In this instance the theme of the double has been used to represent the perfection and nobility of the work of art which survives the creator and his corruptibility.

The Strange Case of Dr Jekyll and Mr Hyde by R. L. Stevenson (1886) is undoubtedly the most popular and imaginative example of this kind of literature. The tale hinges on the struggle between good and evil in the human soul. Dr Jekyll is kind and humane to such a degree that he cannot tolerate the tension between his mind and his instincts and therefore invents a mysterious drug that enables him to suppress at will the side of his nature that threatens the other. In this way he can be in turn the good, kind, helpful doctor his neighbours have come to respect, or the frightful disruptive beast he harbours within him. Unfortunately the scheme gets out of hand: the evil self gradually gains the upper hand and takes over spontaneously, regardless of the mysterious drug. The story ends with the suicide of Dr Jekyll who has become incapable of restraining the evil being to whom he himself had given free expression.

The recurrent theme of these novels is that of the dual personality. It is important to note that the main characters are always highly respectable persons — priests (in *Le*

Somnambule by Mintorn), judges (in *L'Altro* by Landau), virtuous young girls about to take holy orders (*Soeur Marthe* by Ephyre), or daughters of distinguished families (*Minnie Prandon* by Hennique). The list is endless.

In Freudian terms one could say that authors and readers were conscious that the more violent and destructive the repression, the more violent and destructive the force of the repressed. Indeed we are confronted with an extensive cast of respectable characters who were magically transformed into criminals, murderers and prostitutes, compelled by invisible forces to contend with violent and uncontrollable urges which they did with varying degrees of success. However, troubled contemporary consciences could take comfort from the fact that if such things did occur outside the pages of fiction they were the exception, and the victims were already prone to psychic disorders or under the influence of mysterious drugs, infusions, curses, or the hypnotic sway of some evil person.

The good child

Thus it was common knowledge that there was an unconscious part of the self, indeed the notion had been somewhat overexposed. It was Freud's attitude to the subject which caused a scandal. He considered that the mechanisms which trigger off phenomena of an exceptional nature, and which can in certain cases give rise to pathological and abnormal behaviour, are common to all people, and, what is more, are developed in earliest infancy, within the nuclear family which was supposed to be a fortress and buffer against the dangers of the outside world.

During the latter part of the nineteenth century the idealization of childhood had reached its peak: to the extent that

Flaubert in his *Dictionary of Platitudes* ironically recommends, under the entry *Children*, that we should make a great show of affection for them in public. An amusing example of this can be found in a poem I came upon by chance in an Italian gift-book for the year 1865 dedicated to 'The Ladies', that is, the respectable mothers of noble families, where between floral decorations and flourishes a father has immortalized his boundless love:

> Babble, oh Babe,
> Your voice for me
> Equals the harmonies
> Of the harp's throb.
>
> When my heart aches
> With unspent anguish
> Your sweet babble
> Will still it soon.
>
> If your small fist
> Chances to stroke me,
> Grabs at my hair,
> Clings to my hand,
>
> Such bliss then fills me
> As though the dew
> Dropped down from Heaven
> To bathe my breast.
>
> Your breath is fragrant
> As the Spring breeze
> That hovers round
> A bright flower's calyx;
>
> Your mouth's a precious
> Comb of honey.
> I faint with joy
> At your lips' touch.
>
> (Translator's version)

Thus the child is a source of ineffable delight for its parents, a limpid spring at which to restore their flagging energies, a creature of angelic innocence so sexually unaware that passion can be squandered upon it with impunity.

In this way the idealization of childhood reinforces the image of the ideal adult. But in order to give substance to this vision the parents must surround the child not only with love and tenderness but also with care and discipline, so that from being an 'innocent babe' he will develop into a 'respectable citizen', possessing all the requisite qualities. For it is the responsibility of parents from the very beginning to form his personality in the most socially useful way.

The naughty child

Thus if, as Flaubert suggests, it was correct to make a great show of affection in public, in private the child was subjected to the severest educational methods ranging from corporal punishment to the withholding of pleasures (no pudding, no supper, etc.) and to a systematic reign of terror as a means of enforcing parental discipline.

Hoffmann's *Struwwelpeter* was one of the most popular children's books of the time, and it demonstrates vividly how parents feared the appearance of flaws in the characters of their children, and were determined to put them on their guard. In this still widely read book the unfortunate heroes — or victims — of Hoffmann's short stories in verse meet with the most terrible fates (they are burned alive, torn to pieces by dogs, swallowed by fish, have their fingers cut off, are scalded with soup, etc.) for committing the most trivial of childish offences (disobedience, daydreaming, bad manners, etc.). The most savagely punished faults were those most offending the contemporary notions of virtue: disobedience as opposed to respect for authority, daydreaming rather than hard work, a lack of 'good manners'.

The outcome of an education where the rule of fear was an excuse for sadistic tyranny, together with the aggressiveness of its victims, is ironically portrayed in the equally popular *Max und Moritz* by the German Wilhelm Busch (1865). Freud was familiar with this book which tells in intentionally horrifying terms the story of two naughty boys and the tricks they play on the inhabitants of a peaceful village. Hardworking housewives, skilled tailors and respectable schoolmasters are all ruthlessly tormented by the terrible brothers whose sole aim is to humiliate their betters in a sadistic fashion. To this end they mete out death and destruction until the poor victims are themselves caught up in the vicious circle, and become in their turn ferocious persecutors, whereupon, to the relief of all concerned, the mischief-makers are ground to chaff in a millhopper and fed to the geese.

Today educational methods such as these seem totally repugnant, as they must have done to the author who obviously wrote tongue-in-cheek. But the late nineteenth-century parent (though doubtless never guilty of the extremes of cruelty described in *Max und Moritz*) considered the 'wicked tendencies' he observed in his child to be repulsive, and consequently every effort made by tutors and families to repress them was considered to be not only legitimate but necessary.

A digression

This attitude of mind has a long history which we will not go into here. It is, however, important to note that childhood and family life have evolved greatly over the centuries. The Italian social historian Philippe Ariès notes that although the family plays a very important part in modern industrial societies this was not so in earlier times. Basing his study on iconography and the evidence of dress, games and diaries, he claims that in the Middle Ages — which he takes as the starting-point of his research — the idealization of childhood was unheard of. This does not imply that children were not loved: the current attitude was not one of indifference but of non-differentiation. Children under five years of age were not considered to have a specific personality. They were clothed, played with, spoken to, but clothes, games and modes of expression took no account of the child's specific nature and his difference from adults. Very young babies, who were not yet able to take part in the life led by adults, received very little attention. The custom of entrusting babies to wet-nurses during early infancy was widespread; it relieved the wealthier mother from the fatigue of breastfeeding and rearing her babies, and it enabled working class women to carry on with their bread-winning. Owing to the difficult living conditions of the time, and to an almost total lack of knowledge about medicine or hygiene, the infant mortality rate was very high; and it is possible that this emotional detachment on the part of the parents was a kind of safeguard against the pain of repeated bereavement.

Traces of this archaic attitude towards children survived as late as the eighteenth century, and if the child managed to reach the so-called 'age of reason', that is, six or seven, he was still considered to be merely a second-class adult. 'Time alone can cure infancy and youth which are in every respect imperfect conditions', declared the Jesuit Father Baltasar Gracian in 1723.

Montaigne, the great essayist of the Enlightenment, ob-served that he failed to understand how anyone could love a newborn baby passionately when it lacked all spiritual feel-ing, and did not even have an identifiable physical form that might make it worth loving. He too said that he did not wish his children to be nursed by their mother at home. Philippe de Coulanges, a highly educated cousin of Madame de Sévigné, expressed his astonishment at having come across some otherwise sane people who wrote letters to children aged three when even at four they cannot read. He admonished parents that there are few more repulsive sights than that of little children sitting in a row at the dining table, snotty-nosed, dribbling and poking their fingers into every dish. In his opinion children should eat on their own, with a strict governess to teach them how to behave, since they take a long time to learn manners.

But precisely at this time, and because of this fastidiousness, more attention began to be paid to children, and efforts were made to find more suitable methods of educating them. Children began to be taken more seriously, not simply fondled and treated as playthings. Their unformed minds had to be developed, they must become responsible beings and good Christians. In the latter half of the eighteenth century the family began to take on a form not unlike that of today, at least in the middle and upper middle classes, although not among the aristocracy or the masses. The family became a relatively restricted nucleus in which the parents assumed a certain responsibility for their children's education and up-bringing.

Recent historico-sociological research confirms Ariès's theory and extends its scope to include the lower classes. In *The Making of the Modern Family* (1976) Edward Shorter studies the evolution of the family over the past three centuries and stresses the importance of the mother—child relationship as the keystone in the structure of the modern family. In *The Myth of Motherhood* (1981) Elizabeth Badinter shows how the cult of maternal love has varied, and suggests that it reached its peak in the late nineteenth century.

The middle class family

Thus the typical middle class family of the mid-nineteenth century as described by Stifter respects the notion of *domesticas,* of the family circle in which each member had a well-defined role. This family, therefore, represents the climax of an extremely long and complicated evolutionary process. It hinges on the parent—child relationship with an ever-increasing stress on the child's importance: he assumes a central position in the family because of his very existence, and his consequent physical need for hygiene, clothing, food, a better standard of living; and his spiritual need for education and moral supervision — the latter requiring the pitiless suppression of any evil tendencies, bad habits and undesirable companions. He must also be brought up to be a decent citizen, hence the efforts of the family and society to teach him order and obedience.

Whether one took the view that adult wisdom was the only safeguard of a child's innocence, or, in the wake of Rousseau, that children were naturally good and only needed to be protected from misguided notions and encouraged in their natural development, this educative process was firmly entrusted to the parents and carried out within the family circle as if it were a precious conquest.

The Austrian family

For specific historical and cultural reasons the middle class Austrian family was particularly preoccupied with such matters as rank and order; their very homes had to reflect a sense of decorum, of respectability and calm. Claudio Magris has noted an exact parallel between the political order desired by Franz-Josef — stifling state control based on rigidity and regulations, obedience and loyalty to the supranational ideal — and a private life-style characterized by an immutable respect for tradition, a cautious rejection of emotions and feelings, and a suspicion of anything irrational or instinctive which might ruffle the appearance of calm so essential to the Empire's stability.

In Habsburg Austria the bureaucrats formed the framework of this dull and cautious order. 'The figure of the bureaucrat epitomized the spirit of the Empire, his sytem of government and rigid values proof against explosive unrest and the dynamic progress of events. The favourite hero of Austrian literature is the diligent retired civil servant whose only aim in life is to clamp down the wild winds with office paper clips' (Magris, *Il mito asburgico*, p. 22, translator's version).

In *The Radetzky March* Joseph Roth gives a vivid picture of the life-style of an Austrian family of the period. He describes the relationship between the civil servant von Trotta and his young son, Karl Joseph: the fine mesh of strict habits that restrains mutual affection and reduces it to empty ritual, the respect for convention in place of a real sense of values, the wilfully blind faith in the indestructibility of the imperial order, matched by an equally blind faith in the indestructibility of the family hierarchy. In this the father is responsible for his son's future which was determined once and for all at his birth, and the son is responsible to the father for the execution of a programme which makes no allowances for doubt or discussion, and certainly not for outright rebellion.

In this book the gradual disintegration of public values is reflected in the gradual disintegration of private values. When the rigid framework of habit begins to crack, values and affections gradually lose all vitality. With forceful irony Roth depicts the blind tenacity of von Trotta senior, the priest officiating over domestic ritual: meals are always served in the same order and made with the same ingredients and sauces; servants and governess are treated like robots whose only purpose in life is to reflect the daily repetition of the small-scale family drama. He describes von Trotta's obsessive observance of daily habits: his walk in the park, his game of chess in the usual café, his formal conversations with his inferiors. Above all he depicts von Trotta's relationship with his son Karl Joseph whose military career had been decided at birth so that he could represent the family ideals of honour and courage by serving the Emperor. But like Karl Josef's grandfather the legendary hero of the Battle of Solferino, who by pure chance happened to save the Emperor's life, but who was in fact only an ordinary soldier, so too the Habsburg ideal turns out to be an illusion flying in the face of history, 'a worm-eaten house' doomed to decay.

Within the context of this dual political and domestic disintegration, the father's relationship with his son resembles a stage performance that must maintain its formal perfection in order to be credible. The son's automatic 'Yes, Father' and Trotta senior's regular letters punctuate their mutual estrangement. Yet when the collapse of the Empire brings down with it the old order of things this little domestic world takes on in contrast an air of sacred and poetic splendour. In comparison with the unstable tormented world outside, this example of *domesticitas* seems to provide the one fixed point of stability, private affection the only harbour from the political storm and family respectability with its predetermined roles the only source of self-respect.

These roles were very clearly defined. The men were financially responsible for the well-being of the family, and for maintaining its middle class sense of decorum: that is, providing it with a comfortable house, the requisite number of servants and rooms variously allocated for study, entertaining and for intimate family gatherings. The excessive quantity of furniture, knick-knacks, *objets d'art*, paintings and portraits bore witness to the owner's social standing, and to his desire that his house should be a sanctuary for those nearest to him and for their memories of him, a sort of private stronghold and buffer against the ever-changing outside world.

Maintaining the family's air of bourgeois respectability was a source of constant preoccupation, as may clearly be seen from Freud's own letters to his fiancée. In these he constantly reiterates his fear of not having enough money and of not being able to reconcile his scientific career with the equally onerous role of husband and father.

To this all-responsible father total unquestioning obedience was due. Man was master in his own home, and his orders must be rigorously carried out by his wife and children. Just as the Habsburg Father enjoyed the implicit faith of his people in the providential far-sightedness he supposedly derived from his holy status, so too the *pater familias* was trusted and respected. It is not hard to imagine the emotional difficulties in a relationship based on such rigid hierarchical lines and the conflicts between this despotic concept of authority and the individual members of the family.

In his 'Letter to his Father' Franz Kafka describes the anguish of a son whose self-respect is constantly crushed under the weight of his father's importance and who sees no way of escape from his conflicting feelings — of aggression towards a father determined to shape his life without trying to understand his problems, and of guilt at his own powerless aggressiveness which finally paralyses him completely. The focal point of Freud's work is the *Oedipus complex,* that is, the ambivalent love-hate relationship with the father figure. He sees the lack of a positive solution to this complex as the source of neurosis. The mother and wife had the equally onerous role of guardian of rightful affections, educator of children, comforter of the old and sick and an example to all. Freud's early writings include accounts of clinical cases involving the pathology of hysterics who consulted him. With the vividness of a contemporary novelist he describes the dramatic conflicts of women torn between the role assigned to them in all its inherent dignity and self-abnegation, and their very human passions and desires, which a repressive society condemned relentlessly, and which they themselves condemned, being the unconscious heirs to a sense of guilt and self-accusation.

These studies emphasize the price these women had to pay

for their sense of duty to the family and society which narrowly restricted their personalities, and for the powerful inhibitions which prevented them from freeing themselves from these restrictions. Nervous disorders expressed as hysterical symptoms were their only means of escape when social and domestic duty bound them.

In *Studies on Hysteria* Breuer describes the case of Anna O.:

> She was markedly intelligent, with an astonishingly quick grasp of things and penetrating intuition. She possessed a powerful intellect which would have been capable of digesting solid mental pabulum and which stood in need of it — though without receiving it after she had left school . . . The element of sexuality was astonishingly undeveloped in her. [Both Freud and Breuer only realized later that this sexuality was only firmly repressed and not underdeveloped.] . . . This girl, who was bubbling over with intellectual vitality led an extremely monotonous existence in her puritanically minded family. She embellished her life in a manner which probably influenced her decisively in the direction of her illness, by indulging in systematic day-dreaming which she described as her 'private theatre'. (Standard edn, vol. II, pp. 21–2)

Emmy von N. consulted Freud at the age of 41: despite her serious hysterical condition she was leading an apparently 'sane and responsible' life. Since the death of her husband 14 years previously she had managed a large industrial firm, supervised her daughter's education and corresponded with eminent intellectuals. But she had had to spend countless nights by the sick-beds of her husband, her brother and a seriously disturbed psychotic daughter. Freud saw her illness also as the result of a conflict between her passionate disposition — she could be very emotional — and a compulsive reserve imposed on her by her role, her circumstances and by the socially accepted image of the dignified widow and mother, all of which weighed upon her and deprived her of any means of openly acknowledging her needs, even under hypnosis.

> It has also struck me that amongst all the intimate information given me by the patient there was a complete absence of the sexual element, which is, after all, more liable than any other to provide occasion for traumas. It is impossible that her excitations in this field can have left no trace whatsoever; what I was allowed to hear was no doubt an *editio in usum Delphi* [a bowdlerized edition] of her life-story. The patient behaved with the greatest and to all appearances with the most unforced sense of propriety, without a trace of prudishness. When, however, I reflect on the reserve with which she told me under hypnosis about her maid's little adventure in the hotel, I cannot help suspecting that this woman who was so passionate and so capable of strong feelings had not won her victory over her sexual needs without severe struggles, and that at times her attempts at suppressing this most powerful of all instincts had exposed her to severe mental exhaustion. She once admitted to me that she had not married again because, in view of her large fortune, she could not credit the dis-interestedness of her suitors and because she would have reproached herself for damaging the prospects of her two children by a new marriage. (Ibid., p. 103)

The case of Elizabeth von R. was similar to that of the two former patients. Her life was one long history of self-sacrifice and painful experiences, of instincts repressed for the sake of a social image that had to be preserved, of filial devotion that was stronger than the satisfaction of more legitimate desires, of a crippling sense of guilt about sexual fantasies involving her brother-in-law, and, once again, of that unflinching dedication to sick relatives (an adored father, a blind mother and a sister). In each case the death of a loved one totally disrupted the psychic equilibrium of these sacrificial victims to domestic duty.

Elizabeth was intelligent and ambitious. She was passionately fond of her father with whom she had a very close rapport.

> Although the girl's mind found intellectual stimulation from
> this relationship with her father, he did not fail to observe that
> her mental constitution was on that account departing from
> the ideal which people like to see realized in a girl. He
> jokingly called her 'cheeky' and 'cock-sure', and warned her
> against the habit of regardlessly telling people the truth; and
> he often said she would find it hard to get a husband. She was
> in fact greatly discontented with being a girl. She was full of
> ambitious plans. She wanted to study or to have a musical
> training, and she was indignant at the idea of having to
> sacrifice her inclinations and her freedom of judgement by
> marriage. As it was, she nourished herself on her pride in her
> father and in the prestige and social position of her family, and
> she jealously guarded everything that was bound up with
> these advantages. The unselfishness, however, with which she
> put her mother and elder sisters first, when an occasion arose,
> reconciled her parents completely to the harsher side of her
> character. (Ibid., pp. 207–8)

Freud and the concept of infancy

Freud analysed the development of the personality within
families in contemporary society. He attacked at its source
the process of idealization that exalted the parents as guardians
and propagators of 'noble sentiments' on the one hand, and
the child as the fount of human goodness on the other, and he
undertook a critical scientific study of the effect of the family
on its individual members.

Obviously people were not unaware of the influence of the
family on the individual, but Freud's theory was revolutionary
in that he believed that the family formed an intrinsic part of

the individual's character and future existence, not simply as a social institution like any other, but as an 'inner reflection' of the particular family on the particular individual. Through the specific relationship which Freud established between analyst and patient, critical moments in the patient's existence gradually came to light, of which he himself was unaware and which he could not therefore talk about (man is not even master in his own house). From his clinical cases Freud was able to put together the theory that the essential features of a person's character, and the reasons for any subsequent deviance, are established in early childhood and in relationships within the family.

Freud's research showed that from birth human nature is far from being angelic and innocent, indeed it harbours the most violent impulses, particularly aggressive and sexual ones, and any educational method that ignores these impulses, and either thoughtlessly reinforces them or blindly represses them, can be damaging.

The main distinction between Freud's image of man and that on which the repressive ethic of the period was based consists in his view that these infantile impulses are normal. What is more, they constitute a valuable resource which should be exploited, not prematurely destroyed.

According to Johannes Cremerius, author of a book on education and psychoanalysis, the theory of psychoanalysis maintains that from birth man is intent on the satisfaction of his impulses, and his life is ruled by the pleasure principle. To become a civilized member of society he (or his ego) has to learn to control his impulses (or his id). There seems nothing new in this since it is evidently derived from the principles of Western Christianity. What is new is Freud's reassessment of our impulses, and his concept of the notion of control. When Freud calls our impulses a 'valuable resource' he is emphasizing that they should not be suppressed before the individual has exploited them (in contrast with medieval theologians, who thought that human impulses were of a diabolical nature). The child should learn to understand his impulses and so use them for his future benefit. In Freud's view these instincts are the first buddings of sexuality and they determine the course of our adult sexual life.

The main distinction between these two views of human nature is that the educative principles of the one obstruct our undertanding of our normal instincts and seek to repress them from the start, while the other advocates that we develop them until we have reached maturity. In the first case education is seen as the training of an individual to repress his natural instincts, in the second it is seen as the training of an individual to learn how to master them.

Deviants

Pathologists and sexologists of the period were in no way unaware of the fact that human nature can present anomalies and distortions. Krafft-Ebing's *Psycopathia Sexualis* (1866) — an attempt, subsequently revised in several editions, to classify sexual abnormalities on the basis of clinically observed cases — made quite a stir in Freud's day. But by and large such abnormalities were seen either as congenital (that is, as part of the patient's genetic heritage) or as something to which even normal people were subject, but only in very special circumstances. Freud's unacceptable hypothesis was that normal sexuality developed during *normal* childhood from *normal* impulses each of which might become a perversion only if it was not subjected to a process of maturing and integration.

As Freud himself says in *An Autobiographical Study*:

The detaching of sexuality from the genitals has the advantage of allowing us to bring the sexual activities of children and of perverts into the same scope as those of normal adults. The

sexual activities of children have hitherto been entirely neglected and though those of perverts have been recognized it has
been with moral indignation and without understanding.
(Standard edn, vol. XX, p. 38)

Freud's approach to the problem of deviants differed from
the outset in the way in which he related it to his discovery of
a specific infantile sexuality which was different from adult
sexuality yet linked to it by an unbroken thread throughout
its complex evolution. By defining and identifying the various
stages of this evolution, by relating the origins of deviations
to the mutation of a process that occurs in every individual,
whether sane or not, according to a mechanism which is
common to all, by defining through clinical observation the
changes impulses undergo in their intricate progress towards
sexual maturity, he saw mental illness in a different perspective from that of his predecessors. He opened the way to a
study of deviations which had nothing to do with the system
of classification previously used. His approach opposes the
'psychiatric segregation' of the patient, that is, the definition
of certain forms of behaviour as abnormal in so far as they are
incomprehensible to normal people in general; he opposes
too the subsequent diagnosis of an illness which may be
considered the cause of this abnormality based on this
incomprehensibility. This is what distinguishes Freud most
forcibly from the culture of his own time and links him to
ours.

Because the main preoccupation of modern psychiatry is to
arrive at an understanding of the patient, in order to distinguish it from the traditional discipline it has been called
antipsychiatry, an ambiguous term that has given rise to a
certain amount of confusion. This is how the psychiatrist
R. D. Laing, one of the leading exponents of this approach,
deals with the subject of psychiatric patients in his book
Sanity, Madness and the Family, in which he discusses a series

of experiments he made on schizophrenic families. He states
in the introduction:

> In this book, we believe that we show that the experience and
> behaviour of schizophrenics is much more socially intelligible
> than has come to be supposed by most psychiatrists.
>
> We have tried in each single instance to answer the question:
> to what extent is the experience and behaviour of that person,
> who has already begun a career as a diagnosed 'schizophrenic'
> patient, intelligible in the light of the praxis and process of his
> or her family nexus? (p. 27)

We are not trying to prove that there exists a link between
the Freudian method which involves an analyst—patient
relationship and Laing's method which is based on a socio-
phenomenological approach. Nor do we want to show that
Freud anticipated that movement which maintains that a
specific political order can influence the fate of an individual
and whether or not he is 'abnormal'. What concerns us here is
to draw attention to a psychiatric approach which seeks to
understand, and which is diametrically opposed to that of the
academic psychiatry of Freud's time and of today which
seeks merely to classify and distinguish.

In *Politics of the Family* Laing gives an exhaustive account
of a classified case diagnosed and treated by Morel, a famous
psychiatrist who practised in France in Freud's day and was
considered one of the foremost European authorities in the
field of mental illness. This case, reported and analysed by
Laing, highlights the basic difference of approach that we
wish to illustrate.

Laing quotes the whole of Morel's report as published in a
treatise on mental illness in 1860. In brief, a 13-year-old boy,
the son of one of Morel's childhood friends, comes to consult
him. The father is worried about the boy's mental health
since a 'violent hatred for the author of his days has unexpectedly replaced his tender affection'. Morel is most

struck by the fact that the boy's physical growth appears to have been arrested. Indeed, although he is fine-featured and of above-average intelligence, he is extremely small. The boy seems to be mortified by his lack of height, but does not appear in the least concerned about his loathing for his father.

Morel's diagnosis and treatment are related to organic insufficiency: the boy is sent to a hydro-therapeutic institute where he does gymnastics, bathes and undergoes massage. The result is satisfactory from a purely physical point of view, but psychologically the boy seems to withdraw into himself, to lose interest in his studies and to become apathetic. At this point *dementia praecox* (as cases of schizophrenia were then called) — is the label attached to this otherwise incomprehensible development. The fact that the boy's mother was also 'deranged' and his grandmother 'eccentric' appears to confirm the diagnosis. Morel's account ends here. But this is what Laing has to say:

This elegant, concise clinical description is the prototype for what must be millions of comparable diagnoses under comparable circumstances in the last 100 years.

With inessential changes, the structure in this presentation is still the paradigm of most clinical psychiatric examination diagnoses, and treatment of a 'case'.

The complaint is by an 'unhappy father' of a family Morel knew well. The complaint is that the son (aged 13 or 14) had 'suddenly' evidenced to the father 'a violent hatred' of him; whereas before, his father had had the impression that his son held 'the most tender sentiments' towards him. Morel's first comment *on the situation* is exclusively about the boy, not even about the whole boy: his head was well formed and intellectually he was above average. However, he was smaller than average. Such is the spell Morel casts, we may already regard this information as beginning to confirm a diagnosis the great clinician will lead us towards step by step by a process of exclusion, as a detective leads us to a criminal.

Clearly there is nothing the matter with the father. That goes without saying. If the boy, according to the father, hates him, there *must* be something the matter with the boy. His head *looks* all right, and he is doing well at school. But he is rather short. Aha! ... an arrest of development of an inherited constitutional nature. His chief source of misery appears to be that he is small. Aha! This has nothing to do with what is *really* the matter with him, namely, the fact that he hates his father. He has lost his gaiety, he has become sombre, taciturn, and shows a tendency to solitariness. A picture takes shape. Indeed, a new psychiatric syndrome is about to be invented. Sudden onset; the affects attacked first; evidence of a constitutional arrest of development ... *must* be inherited. To clinch it, it does not appear to be caused by onanism (masturbation). And his mother and his grandmother showed signs of mental disorder. There is no question about it. He needs *treatment*. Immediatedly.

... Why does he hate his father and why had he even thought of killing him? We shall never know.

The direct effect, and intention, of psychiatric intervention is to turn this young man into a 'young invalid': to *invalidate* his hatred of his father, under the name of treatment ...

Most psychiatrists among the comparative few who have studied families directly, have come to the view that much psychiatric practice remains as naive as Morel's. (pp. 71—5)

Freud as example

We have so far stressed two aspects of Freud's work: his new concept of infancy and the part played by parents, and his new approach to the problem of deviants, that is, to those who present a certain deviation or abnormality in their behaviour or psychological make-up.

These two aspects are closely related and we see them as being particularly important. In his attitude to them Freud is closest to our own culture and furthest from his own. It will thus be easier for us to understand how hard it was for Freud himself to overcome his personal resistance to some of the things he gradually discovered in the course of his clinical observations. It will also explain why, when studying the theory of 'trauma' in hysteric patients — the theory, that is, of an actual rape experience having taken place in the patient's childhood with detrimental consequences — Freud had been reluctant to formulate the disturbing theory of the presence of sexual impulses in the young child, of their intricate development within the family and of the unconscious encouragement they receive from the very parents who are officially entrusted with the education and protection of 'innocent' children. Thus the crucial importance which Freud attached to sexuality and especially to infantile sexuality was by no means a preconceived idea. On the contrary, it was something he was very reluctant to recognize, which forced him, almost beyond his personal limits and against his prejudices, to attack the ideological framework of his time, his class and his culture. Only his unquenchable thirst for knowledge, his exceptional scientific integrity and his stubborn hunt after truth could have led Freud to explore the unknown territory of the unconscious.

2

Vienna, the Contradictory City

Vivacious Vienna

We have described the conservative middle class Vienna in which Freud was born and in which he brought up his own family. To his many sons and daughters he was a conscientious and hard-working father, constantly weighed down by the responsibility of supporting his dependants financially. As a scientist he was singularly at odds with the ideological conventions of his time, and with whatever traces of these he had unconsciously inherited. This contradiction undoubtedly existed within him and is further evidence of his unique ability as a scientist to dissociate himself from his own inner conflicts through his remarkable integrity and the nature of the psychoanalytical method itself.

Freud, like many other prominent Austrians, especially those of Vienna in the mid-nineteenth century, was a profoundly tormented man. Society as a whole was torn betwen a tendency to cling to the 'good old days' and the attraction of conflicting revolutionary forces; it was caught between nostalgia and rejection, between the fascination of the Habsburg myth and the slings and barbs which exposed the paradox, the hypocrisy and the unhealthy division which lay below its highly polished veneer.

The image of Vienna as a staid and stifling capital is at odds with the popular image of a vivacious city of waltzes, cafés, street music, colourful military parades, sophisticated court balls and romantic plays in which love is not all ecstasy and tormented passion but a playful and stimulating ingredient in the theatre of life itself. Magris quotes a description of this alternative Vienna by the writer and dramatist Heinrich Laube:

> How meaningless my past life seemed to me at that moment with its erudition, its theories, its restlessness and libertarianism. 'Good God, I said to myself, what is the point of all these complications? . . . Here is true earthly felicity . . . to go down into the street, kiss the girls and eat a nice fried chicken, what business is it of yours how the world goes? . . . In no other city is it so easy to do nothing and to think of nothing . . . This city is a paradise without fig-leaves, serpent or tree of knowledge. It is a wonder that manna doesn't fall from the skies and good wine gush out of the gutter. (*Il mito asburgico*, p. 76, translator's version)

Two sides to the coin

Here then are two very different and equally well-documented faces of Vienna.

Claudio Magris, who is the most perceptive critic of Austrian literature of this period, sought an explanation for this duality in its historical and political background:

> The last phase of the Habsburg civilization seemed to be poised between two contrasting poles, between the nostalgic awareness of its own decline which it endures with silent dignity, and the thoughtless light-heartedness of an operetta. The Emperor's tedious old age symbolises the Habsburg decline and epitomises the pathetic stoicism with which the monarchy of the Danube withstood the blows which rained

down on it. 'I am spared absolutely nothing' Franz Josef would sigh in the face of repeated domestic and political mishaps, echoing the passive tragedy of the *finis Austriae,* and somehow investing this attitude with a dignified sense of duty.

At the same time this dying world is masquerading in fancy dress, disguising its decline with a sparkling zest for life and escaping into a superficial, careless sensuality. The muddy yellow Danube turns blue, and historical and political disaster are forgotten in a fleeting, sentimental and self-indulgent paradise. The Emperor's painful pedantry may give the impression of ordered restraint but his braided uniform and general ostentation speak of the grandeur of court balls, sumptuous coaches and glittering officers. Novels, plays, poetry and music recreate the delicate unmistakable features of the Vienna of waltzes, of light, sentimental love-affairs, of the love of life itself — indeed of a *belle époque* less unbridled than in Paris, perhaps, but more light-hearted. (Ibid., p. 185)

Vienna in decline is like a cracked mirror that cannot reflect a true image, and therefore appears fragmented and inconsistent. Thus the city of Vienna, the precious pearl in the Habsburg crown which was so dear to the Emperor's heart, was the place above all others whose inhabitants lived a life of inconsistencies and false appearances.

It has been said that Vienna was the city of paradoxes; certainly many mutually incompatible political and ideological movements were initiated there: Zionism and anti-Semitism; the cult of traditional womanhood and feminism; the aristocratic ostentation of state occasions and the prototype of the capitalist bourgeoisie not entirely free of a staid Biedermeier cautiousness; a flourishing middle class with values still apparently rooted in the past, and a restless coterie of equally middle class intellectuals profoundly antagonistic to these values. This was the Vienna where science thrived and was discussed by a wide variety of learned societies. Even

Doctor Freud was invited after due consideration to speak about his research into the role of sexuality. His lecture was considered 'wonderful' by two members of the Philosophical Society who were invited to Freud's house to hear him give a preliminary reading of it, but:

> The lecture was therefore arranged for the fourth week. A few hours beforehand, however, I received an express letter saying that some members had objected after all and asking me to be kind enough to start by illustrating my theory with inoffensive examples and then announce that I was coming to objectionable matter and make a pause, during which the ladies could leave the hall. Of course I immediately cried off, and the letter in which I did so at any rate did not lack pepper and salt. Such is scientific life in Vienna! (*The Origins of Psycho-Analysis,* p. 329)

This was the Vienna where radically innovative scientific discoveries (of which psychoanalysis was certainly one) were greeted with a conspiracy of silence, unless whoever had pioneered them was officially acknowledged by bureaucracy and society.

In a letter to his friend Fliess, Freud gives an account of his long-awaited nomination to a professorship; a nomination which had the backing of authoritative scientists such as Notnagel and Krafft-Ebing but had been repeatedly turned down by the Minister of Education and was finally granted only after the intervention of a mutual acquaintance and Freud's donation of a valuable painting to the Gallery of Modern Art in which the minister took a particular interest:

> So one day my patient came to her appointment beaming and waving an express letter from the Minister. It was done. The *Wiener Zeitung* has not yet published it, but the news spread quickly from the Ministry. The public enthusiasm is immense. Congratulations and bouquets keep pouring in, as if the role

of sexuality had been suddenly recognized by His Majesty, the interpretation of dreams confirmed by the Council of Ministers, and the necessity of the psycho-analytic therapy of hysteria carried by a two-thirds majority in Parliament. (Ibid., p. 344)

In *The Man Without Qualities* Robert Musil gives an ironic description of Austria's gift for inconsistency:

On paper it called itself the Austro-Hungarian Monarchy; in speaking, however, one referred to it as Austria, that is to say, it was known by a name that it had, as a State, solemnly renounced by oath, while preserving it in all matters of sentiment, as a sign that feelings are just as important as constitutional law and that regulations are not the really serious thing in life. By its constitution it was liberal, but its system of government was clerical. The system of government was clerical, but the general attitude to life was liberal. Before the law all citizens were equal but not everyone, of course, was a citizen. There was a parliament, which made such vigorous use of its liberty that it was usually kept shut; but there was also an emergency powers act by means of which it was possible to manage without parliament, and every time when everyone was just beginning to rejoice in absolutism, the Crown decreed that there must now again be a return to parliamentary government. Many such things happened in this State, and among them were those national struggles that justifiably aroused Europe's curiosity and are today completely misrepresented. They were so violent that they several times a year caused the machinery of State to jam and come to a dead stop. But between whiles, in the breathing-spaces between government and government, everyone got on excellently with everyone else and behaved as though nothing had ever been the matter. (p. 33)

The deceptive calm in Austria during the last decades of the century, with its cultural climate 'still and treacherous as a quagmire', gave way in the first years of the new century to an atmosphere of stimulating excitement bubbling over with new unfocused ideas.

> Nobody knew exactly what was on the way; nobody was able to say whether it was to be a new art, a New Man, a new mentality or perhaps a reshuffling of society. So everyone made of it what he liked. But people were standing up on all sides to fight against the old way of life. Suddenly the right man was on the spot everywhere; and, what is so important, men of practical enterprise joined forces with the men of intellectual enterprise. Talents developed that had previously been choked or had taken no part at all in public life. They were as different from each other as anything well could be, and the contradictions in their aims were unsurpassable. The Superman was adored, and the Subman was adored; health and the sun were worshipped, and the delicacy of consumptive girls was worshipped; people were enthusiastic hero-worshippers and enthusiastic adherents of the social creed of the Man in the Street; one had faith and was sceptical, one was naturalistic and precious, robust and morbid; one dreamed of ancient castles and shady avenues, autumnal gardens, glassy ponds, jewels, hashish, disease and demonism, but also of prairies, vast horizons, forges and rolling-mills, naked wrestlers, the uprisings of slaves of toil, man and woman in the primeval Garden, and the destruction of society. Admittedly these were contradictions and very different battle-cries, but they all breathed the same breath of life. If that epoch had been analysed, some such nonsense would have come out as a square circle supposed to be made of wooden iron; but in reality all this had blended into shimmering significance. This illusion, which found its embodiment in the magical date of the turn of the century, was so powerful that it made some hurl themselves enthusiastically upon the new, as yet un-trodden century, while others were having a last fling in the old one, as in a house that one is moving out of anyway, without either one or the other party feeling that there was very much difference between the two attitudes. (Ibid., p. 59)

The women of Vienna

The literati of the period have handed down to us their
evidence of these restless times in writing of great quality.
Their female heroines or victims, overstimulated and euphoric
and a prey to light-hearted love-affairs, reflect the ambiguous
interplay of traditional respectability and wayward emotion.
In *The Radetzky March* by Joseph Roth, for instance, the
very young lieutenant Carl Joseph experiences for the first
time passionate feelings for a woman: the tender and maternal
Frau Slama. But his passion is 'convulsively restrained by his
rigid limbs and the solid buttons of his uniform' and sacrificed, or rather 'filed away' after her death, out of an equally
rigid and solid regard for social convention. Or there is the
obliging and no longer youthful Frau Taussig 'who protects
herself against the corrosion of age with the youngest possible males as if they were breakwaters'; while in Musil's *The
Man Without Qualities,* Leontine's lover views her statuesque
beauty with the detached possessiveness of the owner of a
valuable but useless object.

Mitzi Schnagel, the heroine of Roth's *The Thousand and
Second Night,* is the most pathetic and ambiguous example of
the genre: this modest little shop assistant selling clay pipes in
a small provincial town is dazzled by the charms of Captain
Baron Taittinger, and surrenders to him and to all the
disasters that follow with an ecstatic yet passive docility,
being the unwitting cause of his ultimate ruin. If the radiant
Captain had not come into her life little Mitzi would never
have joined the ranks of Viennese prostitutes, those 'poor
game-birds who go willingly in search of the own hunters',
making their choice from a throng of dispossessed aristocrats,
still amply endowed with charm, fine residences, good manners, good clothes and good horses; or from the ranks of
officers in an unemployed army who spend their free time

gambling or making love, always a-glitter in their imperial uniforms and 'dressed up like prostitutes of war'.

Vienna belonged also to the painters, sculptors, writers and playwrights who met at parties or in cafés. They were intolerant of the ruling conventions, keen to denounce their inherent hypocrisy and always ready to begin an affair with one of the pretty middle class hostesses who entertained them in their salons and who 'compensated for the fading of their good looks in the company of brainless lieutenants, coarse businessmen and dull bureaucrats' with a spate of part-erotic, part-intellectual love affairs, like the intrepid Hilde in Roth's *The Silent Prophet*. She is caught pathetically between the first stirrings of feminism and the legacy of an artfully conservative culture:

She was no different from the young women of her time and station. She transformed the submissive romanticism of her mother into an Amazon martiality, demanded the recognition of civil rights, including, in passing as it were, free love. Under the slogan 'Equal rights for all!' the daughters of good homes at that period rushed into life, into the high schools, into railway trains, luxury liners, into the dissecting-room and the laboratory. For them there blew through the world that familiar fresh breeze that every new generation believes it has discovered. Hilde was determined not to surrender herself in marriage. Her 'closest friend' had committed the betrayal of marrying the enormously wealthy Herr G.; she owned carriages, horses, flunkeys, coachmen, liveries. But Hilde, who gladly enjoyed sharing in her friend's wealth and laid claim to the carriages and the liveries for shopping expeditions, asserted: 'Irene's happiness means nothing to me, she has sold her freedom.' The men to whom she said this found her charming, unusually intelligent, delightfully self-willed. And as, on top of this she had a dowry and a father with good connections, one or the other thought of marrying her despite her principled objection, in their old-fashioned masculine way. (p. 54)

Diotima in Musil's *The Man Without Qualities* is intelligent, ambitious, charming and sexually restless, and pursues obsessively her illusion of making her salon the centre of some vast patriotic movement that will translate into concrete terms the spirit of 'old Austrian culture':

> This illusion Diotima called 'culture', and usually, with a special amplification, 'our old Austrian culture'. This was an expression that she had learnt to make more and more frequent use of since her ambition had become spiritualised by expansion. What she meant by it was: the beautiful paintings of Velasquez and Rubens that hung in the Imperial museums; the fact that Beethoven had been to all intents and purposes an Austrian; Mozart, Haydn, the Cathedral of St. Stephen, the Burgtheater; the Court ceremonial heavy with the weight of tradition; the Innere Stadt, the district where the smartest *couturiers* and dress-shops of an empire with fifty million inhabitants were crowded together; the tactful demeanour of high officials; Viennese cookery, the aristocracy, which considered itself second to none except the English, and its ancient palaces; the social tone which was permeated with sometimes genuine, but usually sham, aestheticism. (pp. 115—16)

Diotima assembled in her salon people from the highest social echelons in the vain hope that a gathering of intellectuals and men of action, scientists and bank managers, technicians, politicians, ministers and generals and the inevitable smattering of beautiful women might result in important initiatives being taken.

> It was particularly the women that Diotima made a point of, though giving preference to 'ladies' rather than to 'intellectual women'. 'Life today is overburdened with knowledge', she used to say, 'too much so for us to be able to do without the Integral Woman'. She was convinced that only the Integral

Woman still possessed the magical radiation that could envelop the intellect with the forces of life itself, which, to her way of thinking, the intellect was obviously in dire need of for its salvation. This theory of the enveloping woman and the forces of life redounded, furthermore, much to her credit among those young noblemen who frequented her at-homes because it was considered 'the thing' and also because Permanent Secretary Tuzzi was quite well liked; for the idea of Non-Fractional Life is of course the very thing for the nobility. And, coming down to particularities, Diotima's drawing-room, where one could become absorbed in conversations *à deux* without attracting attention, was, without Diotima's having the slightest notion of it, even more favoured as a place of tender meetings and long heart-to-heart talks than even a church. (Ibid., pp. 114−15)

At this time, Lou Andreas Salome was the leading lady of the European intellectual scene. She inspired Nietzsche and Rilke and later became Freud's pupil, psychoanalyst and the comfort of his old age. She travelled extensively, but most often to Vienna, for she relished its particular combination of the erotic and the intellectual.

Parallels with the present

This then is the cultural soil in which Freud's work took root. While political crises shook authority and social order new voices could be heard in the confusion calling for a fresh code of values. These new values often marked the generation gap between fathers and sons — the former enjoying the benefits of their position within the system and completely identifying with the roles they had assumed; the latter rebellious and restless, already aware that behind the rigid facade lay disintegration and conflict. Although the appearance of stability persisted 'governed by ideological requirements that presided over every manifestation of existence like a police force' (Musil, *The Man Without Qualities*), this stability, on closer inspection, seemed like the sclerosis of an old man unable to change his position rather than the exercise of a superior wisdom. Ever more frequently there was discord between members of the same generation and the same class, if not within the same person. In this respect, the period was similar to our own, and it is therefore no coincidence that the personalities who lent colour to the culture of the time and the writers who recorded and accounted its trials and tribulations still appear surprisingly modern.

Some years ago, in 'Il medioevo già cominciato', Umberto Eco described the circumstances of our disjointed existence in a semi-serious fashion where he compared the disintegration of the Roman Empire in the West to our present predicament. According to him we are experiencing the crisis of Pax Americana, that is, the decline of an age in which a great international power established, or tried to establish, the unification of several nations through language, ideology, art and technology. Spurred on by the 'new barbarians', be they the Chinese, the populations of the Third World, the generation of rebels, or immigrants in big cities, we are heading for that confusion of influences that threatens 'the image of Liberal Managerial English-speaking Man whose original hero was Robinson Crusoe and whose Virgil was Max Weber':

> In his little suburban villa the average crew-cut executive still models himself on the upright Roman, but his son already has an Afro hair-style, wears a Mexican poncho, plays the Asian cyther, reads Buddhist texts or humanist pamphlets and blissfully lumps together Herman Hesse, the Zodiac, alchemy, the Thoughts of Mao, marijuana and urban guerilla methods ... On the other hand the Roman survivor too, when at a loose end, plays at wife-swopping and puts the puritanical image of the family in jeopardy.

As part of a vast corporation (a vast system that is falling apart) this crew-cut Roman is in fact already experiencing total decentralization and the collapse of central authority (or authorities) now reduced to a mere sham, a complex of abortive principles. (p. 121 and *passim*, translator's version)

The same irony, the same bitter awareness of a society disintegrating under a veil of abstruse principles is expressed by the young Habsburg officer Franz Tunda in Joseph Roth's *Flight Without End*. Tunda's inner anxiety condemns him to a life of perpetual wandering in the search for his irretrievably lost identity. He goes to see his brother, the successful conductor of an orchestra in a city on the Rhine who is married to the irreproachable Klara. The conductor's marriage — apart from occasional superficial affairs with admiring females — is like a 'still lake over which blew a constant cool breeze'. His little daughter is a model child: 'she had imbibed her mother's placid unintoxicating milk, and formed her character correspondingly'. The house exudes order, ease and even opulence, Klara's 'social conscience [being] outraged more by the word ['opulence'] than the fact'.

The house is sumptuously and eclectically furnished with Russian icons, samovars, candlesticks and silverware acquired from ruined old Jewish families, and with statutes of Buddha, Roman Catholic church ornaments, Gothic madonnas and modern paintings. Franz Tunda gestures towards the Buddhas, the cushions, the deep wide sofas and oriental carpets, and says to his brother, who thinks to align himself with the culture and ancient traditions of the old bourgeoisie:

Is this European culture? . . . It seems to me that you've borrowed something from other sources as well. Tonight, your guests danced some negro dances which are probably not to be found in Parsifal. I can't understand how you can still speak of German culture. Where is it? In the way the women dress? . . . This ancient culture of yours has developed a thousand holes. You plug the holes by borrowing from

Asia, Africa, America. But the holes go on growing. You retain the European uniform, the dinner-jacket and pale complexion, but you dwell in mosques and Indian temples. If I were you, I should wear a burnous. (p. 90)

In Vienna, in the same way, the 'old bourgeois culture', like Diotima's 'old Austrian culture', has become an abstract principle appended to a decaying society, which remains unaware of the changes it has undergone and which, while hypocritically and superficially respected, is in reality being betrayed. Here a group of young artists, writers and intellectuals known as the Young Viennese group used to meet at the Griensteidl Café. They used their literary gifts and clear-sighted powers of criticism to give a pitiless description of the society they saw crumbling about them. The varied gathering included the ardent polemicist Karl Kraus, founder of *Die Fakel,* the daily paper with which for 30 years he attempted to discredit *Die Neue Freie Presse,* the powerful and official paper of the Habsburg regime; Schnitzler, the doctor and novelist who described middle class Vienna in chilling terms; and the poet and dramatist Hofmannsthal, an aristocrat by birth and education who roundly condemned Vienna's scintillating and vacuous 'high society' with its craving for elegance to the exclusion of all feeling, and its affected emotions which become nothing more than a battle of wits.

Neither reaction nor revolution

All these writers lacked a political sense of direction. Although clearly aware of the disintegration of Habsburg rule and of the futility of its efforts to promote an alliance between the various nations which were already striving for their independence, they had no alternative political purpose or ideal to put forward. As Musil observes, they 'were having a last fling in the old [century], as in a house that one is moving out of anyway'. The main characters in their plays and novels are anti-heroes, that is, they are heroically sincere in the manner in which they stress the negative aspect of their position: either acknowledging that the standards of the past are untenable in the present, or refusing to acknowledge any dignity or worth in the new era.

Even the heroes of Roth's last novels who had had first-hand experience of revolution — Franz Tunda, for instance, in *Flight Without End,* or Friedrich Kargan in *The Silent Prophet* — deny the validity of their experience by their self-destructiveness. Perpetual wanderers and strangers to themselves, they destroy their own identities because that is the only choice they have, since their own authenticity consists solely in being the conscious spectators of the non-being that surrounds them.

Franz Tunda, a young Austrian officer in the First World War, is taken prisoner by the Russians. More or less by chance he joins the ranks of the Revolution when he falls in love with the young revolutionary Natasha, and gradually, despite not having any sincere revolutionary convictions he becomes an active participant. When the armed revolution comes to an end and turns into a laborious civil operation, the ardent flames of love and revolution in Tunda's heart both die away. Estranged from his own past 'as from a country forsaken forever, in which he had spent insignificant years', and from his present, he sets out on a pilgrimage towards the old Europe with no purpose except his own annihilation. The endless journey takes him to Paris: 'It was at this hour that my friend Tunda, thirty-two years of age, healthy and vigorous, a strong young man of diverse talents, stood on the Place de la Madeleine, in the centre of the capital of the world, without any idea what to do. He had no occupation, no desire, no hope, no ambition, and not even any self-love. No one in the whole world was as superfluous as he' (*Flight*

Without End, p. 144). Yet it is precisely his own non-being and that of the world about him that constitutes the only possible reality: 'He lived in an odour of corruption and fed on rottenness, he breathed the dust of disintegrating houses and listened with delight to the song of the woodworms' (ibid., p. 143).

Friedrich Kargan, the hero of *The Silent Prophet*, makes a conscious choice of the revolutionary cause. He has led a clandestine existence, has experienced deportation, the excitement of armed resistance and revolutionary triumph. But he realizes that the new world is modelled on the old; bureaucrats 'like the flocks of crows war and revolution left in their wake' began once again to rule with a relentlessness to which their political commitment adds a certain cruelty; revolutionaries 'like the Jews who always turn towards the East when they pray, always tend towards the right once they have achieved power'; and 'the revolution remains on the left, only its representatives shift to the right'.

To the disillusioned revolutionary the new world is nothing but an incoherent mass of false beliefs; proletarians are training for a revolution that has already misfired; the bourgeoisie are absorbed in their pleasures, the businessmen in their rapacious appropriation of wealth, and the representatives of the old prerevolutionary world who have outlasted their time wander about like ghosts and are treated with 'the courteous respect which is due to ancient and forgotten monuments'.

Kargan, like Tunda, opts for a voluntary exile in Siberia, far from the 'senseless clamour of the present'.

Psychological man

The characters in these novels live out the tragedy which overtook Austrian intellectuals at the turn of the century. The collapse of the political standards of the old world fostered an attitude of solitary indifference and withdrawal, and forced thinking people to examine the hopelessly unbridgeable gap between private needs and public values. As heirs to the liberal bourgeois tradition with its respect for the individual, they focused their attention on the uniqueness of that individual, but he was now an individual less concerned with reality than with himself, discovering in himself the same discrepancy between reason and emotion, between passion and duty and between instinct and ethics.

In a previously quoted passage from *'Fin de Siècle' Vienna: Politics and Culture,* dealing with the relationship between Vienna's political climate and its interest in psychology, Schorske points out that the main theme in art and literature was man's reaction to the declining society in which he found himself. From this emerged a new concept of man: he was no longer *rational man,* a representative of the early middle classes who aimed to create the best of all possible worlds through his scientific mastery of nature and his moral mastery of himself, but *psychological man,* a more interesting but also more dangerous and unpredictable creature. This new man, conscious of his own ambiguity and misery, desiring self-knowledge and aware of the discrepancy between the reality of everyday life and his unconscious dreams, instincts and desires, is central to the work of both Schnitzler and Freud.

Freud—Schnitzler—Hofmannsthal

In a letter Freud wrote to Schnitzler for his sixtieth birthday, Freud, who was six years his senior, made a very private confession:

> I think I have avoided you from a kind of reluctance to meet my double. Not that I am easily inclined to identify myself

with another, or that I mean to overlook the difference in talent that separates me from you, but whenever I get deeply absorbed in your beautiful creations I invariably seem to find beneath their poetic surface the very presuppositions, interests and conclusions which I know to be my own. Your determinism as well as your scepticism — what people call pessimism — your preoccupation with the truths of the unconscious and of the instinctual drives in man, your dissection of the cultural conventions of our society, the dwelling of your thoughts on the polarity of love and death; all this moves me with an uncanny familiarity. (*Letters*, pp. 344—5)

There is indeed an extraordinary affinity between the two men, not simply in their work but also in certain biographical details. They both came from middle class Jewish families; both had opted for a medical career without being quite sure of their choice; both attended the same surgery for nervous diseases where the great Meynert taught, and Bernheim's school at Nancy where hypnosis was scientifically studied. Until the great success of *Anatol* in 1893, when he became a professional playwright and novelist, Schnitzler like Freud wrote articles on hypnosis, telepathy, neuroses and psychotherapy. They both veered dramatically away from their original course of study, though in different directions: Schnitzler abandoned medico-scientific research for literature, Freud for psychology. Even Schnitzler's use of psychoanalytical concepts in his novels and plays follows the same pattern as in Freud's early works (see Kupper and Rollman-Branch, 'Freud and Schnitzler'). Hypnotism and the problems it causes in those who have undergone it and in those to whom it has revealed the dual personality of a loved one is a central theme in *Anatol* (1893) and in *Paracelsus* (1897). The significance of unconscious motivation which is the main theme of Freud's *Studies on Hysteria* (1895) runs through all of Schnitzler's later plays. His ample use of dream material in his books to express repressed or unconscious desires (for

instance, in *Double Dream*), and his use of interior mono-
logue as a literary device (as in *Casanova's Homecoming*,
1918), seems to draw on Freud's interpretation of dreams and
his free association method.

Rather than relate this affinity to a mutual or even one-
sided influence (though we know for certain that they
followed each other's progress with interest), it is more
fruitful to trace it back to their common culture, to their
principal interest in *psychological man* in conflict with society
and with himself. This is the theme of Hofmannsthal's
psychological drama of history and politics, *The Tower*
(1893), which examines the conflict between a father, in this
case a powerful king, and his son, a poet and prophet. The
father is afraid that his son will rebel against the stern and
oppressive rule which he considers necessary in order to
maintain law and order, and so cuts him off from all human
intercourse. But precisely because he is isolated from contact
with power in all its cruelty the son rediscovers in seemingly
inhuman conditions the very root of human good. The son's
tragic end signals defeat for those intellectuals whose dearest
ambition was to reconstruct society on a basis of harmony,
perfection and beauty, but respecting also the needs and
instincts of people which would no longer be condemned by
social convention or rigid rationalism, but instead would be
integrated (Freud would have said sublimated) into a better
scheme of things.

Faced with bourgeois society and the equivocal divide
between its morals and its instincts, Schnitzler limits himself
to describing the insoluble conflict, the blind and often
pernicious game of mutual deceit, and the greater deceit
which man practises on himself when he is ignorant of the
deepest root causes of his behaviour. According to him,
dreaming and waking, reality and fiction are all one, and we
cannot presume to judge whether an action is right or wrong
since we can never fully understand the true motives of our

behaviour. We might not even benefit from being able to delve deep into ourselves to examine why we do what we do, and thus discovering our often guilty intentions. Heinrich in *The Road to the Open* (1908) voices Schnitzler's view:

> You're probably thinking of the fact that I recently drove a creature straight to her death and in spite of that felt, so to speak, quite guiltless . . . Yes. I felt quite guiltless. Somewhere or other in my soul and somewhere else, perhaps deeper down, I felt guilty . . . And deeper down still, guiltless again. The only question is how deep we look down into ourselves. And when we have lit the lights in all the storeys, why we are everything at the same time: guilty and guiltless, cowards and heroes, fools and wise men . . . My look-out is ghastly, you know. You surely must have noticed it before. What's the good to me of the lights burning in all my storeys? What's the good to me of my knowledge of human nature and my splendid intelligence? Nothing . . . Less than nothing. (Translator's version)

Schnitzler stands 'motionless, rigid, half dead' before a shifting world, relying on his literary talent to describe its horrifying ambiguity. Hofmannsthal trusted to the sublime power of art to make sense of the world's inconsistencies — but in his last work, published after the First World War, it is evident that he has come to realize that his utopian dream of universal harmony is unattainable.

Freud

Where did Freud stand in relation to this cultural background? We know that he read a great deal of contemporary fiction, and like every true Viennese citizen was an assiduous theatre-goer. From his birthday letter to Schnitzler we gather that he was not only very well aware of what was happening on the cultural scene but felt a strong affinity with those active in it. He was very strict in his habits both as a man and as a scholar, and in this was the very antithesis of Schnitzler, that *enfant terrible* who was lionized as a playwright by society, while at the same time he carried on numerous love affairs in the dissolute world of the theatre. Freud was also very different from Hofmannsthal, who frequented the aristocracy and had been accustomed from childhood to wealth and luxury, and to the preciousness of life which, as Karl Kraus observed ironically, 'he despised while worshipping all that made it beautiful'. Towards the end of his letter to Schnitzler Freud states that his vocation lies inevitably in research: 'I am inclined to give preference to the explorer. But forgive me for drifting into psychoanalysis; I just can't help it. And I know that psychoanalysis is not the means of gaining popularity' (*Letters*, p. 345). Freud was torn between his affectionate admiration for the poet, and stubborn pride in his own choice of a less popular profession. Thus, while accepting their remarkable similarity, Freud recognizes the way in which he differs from his 'double'.

The fact that he avoided meeting Schnitzler for so many years becomes less difficult to understand when one considers the following passage from 'The "Uncanny"' (1919) in which Freud describes the feelings of anxiety caused by meeting one's double, the uncanny sense that something is being unearthed which should have remained hidden. A confrontation with Schnitzler might have made Freud aware of 'all the unfulfilled but possible futures to which we still like to cling in phantasy, all the strivings of the ego which adverse external circumstances have crushed, and all our suppressed acts of volition which nourish in us the illusion of Free Will' (standard edn, vol. XVII, p. 236). Thus when we are confronted with other people's hopes and aspirations which we recognize as those which we have repressed in ourselves we feel ill at ease. Why was Freud proud of having made a different choice, and why did he persist in pursuing it despite making himself unpopular in the process? Like Schnitzler, Freud exposes and explores the complexities of relationships, but — and in this lies the difference between science and art — Freud looked for the laws governing cause and effect within the chaos of experience. His approach was not the logical positivism of nineteenth-century scientists, which examined concrete data, but a rational approach bordering on the irrational, which acknowledges the deep-rooted influence and potential of the latter, and seeks to make sense of whatever in the individual is *alienated*.

This concept of alienation refers to the inner conflict within the individual who is torn between the *pleasure principle* to which he naturally tends, and which clamours for immediate satisfaction, and the *reality principle* which requires a postponement of satisfaction, the curbing of desires, or their redirection towards more socially acceptable ends; or again — and this is the most negative solution — their repression or actual suppression whereby they are blotted out from consciousness and have to resort to a disguised form of expression. In this conflict which begins in early childhood, the ego must always act as mediator between the demands of the instinct and those of reality. For this reason clinical research, which was Freud's chosen field, must always be complemented by social research.

Man and society

Freud's specific interest in the main ethical and religious movements in societies dates from 1912 with *Totem and Taboo* in which he analyses a community as an entity for the first time. His last work in this field was *Moses and Monotheism,* written between 1934 and 1938. In the intervening years his main works on the subject were: *Group*

Psychology and the Analysis of the Ego (1921) and *Civilization and its Discontents* (1930).

Freud approached these studies in the manner of a clinical investigator rather than a social anthropologist. In other words, he started from the assumption that there was such a thing as a collective psyche, and that it developed along the same lines as the individual psyche obeying the same laws and mechanisms that Freud had discovered in the course of his clinical work.

Civilization and its Discontents is of particular interest here since it is Freud's most exhaustive inquiry into man's relationship with society. It would be presumptuous, he says, to ask the purpose of human existence but, less ambitiously, we can try to find out what people expect of life. They expect to become and remain happy, and they hope to do so either by avoiding pain or by seeking pleasure. There are various ways of avoiding pain, none of which ensures happiness. Freud examines these in turn, detailing their advantages, if any, and stressing their limitations and the risks they may involve.

We may try to damp down or stimulate the senses by the use of various drugs that lessen pain or heighten perception: 'one can at any time withdraw from the pressure of reality and find refuge in a world of one's own with better conditions of sensibility'. But intoxicants which enable one to do this are dangerous and harmful. 'They are responsible, in certain circumstances, for the useless waste of a large quota of energy which might have been employed for the improvement of the human lot' (*Civilization and its Discontents*, standard edn, vol. XXI, p. 78). Or we may suppress our instincts by exerting great self-control, as advocated by certain nineteenth-century ethicists, or practise the kind of detachment prescribed by Eastern philosophers. But while lessening our frustrations, these methods undoubtedly also reduce our capacity for enjoyment.

We can also redirect our desires so that they do not make us feel frustrated with the world, by finding pleasure in some artistic activity, for instance, or in the exercise of a profession of our choice, 'if ... by means of sublimation it makes possible the use of existing inclinations, of persisting or constitutionally reinforced instinctual impulses' (ibid., p. 80n). But obviously this possibility is only open to exceptionally gifted people. Freud is very much aware of the problems arising when people are not able to enjoy their work.

There is a more direct route to pleasure which does not consist simply in avoiding pain or reorientating one's desires, and that is to love and be loved. This is undoubtedly the most satisfying state an individual can achieve, but, as everyone knows, it makes one vulnerable to the worst of all sufferings: a dangerous dependence on the loved one and the possibility of being rejected or separated from him or her by circumstances beyond one's control.

Love has wider implications in establishing and developing human communities, since through feelings of friendship, affection and co-operativeness people may be bound together more strongly than they would be through merely working together or by common necessity. Yet in the course of evolution 'the relation of love to civilization loses its unambiguity. On the one hand love comes into opposition to the interests of civilization; on the other civilization threatens love with substantial restrictions' (ibid., p. 103).

At this point Freud states unambiguously the cause and effects of such restriction. In order to keep going, society requires a large fund of psychic energy which sexuality adequately provides: 'In this respect civilization behaves towards sexuality as a people or a stratum of its population does which has subjected another one to its exploitation. Fear of revolt by the suppressed elements drives it to stricter precautionary measures. A high-water mark in such a development has been reached in our Western European civilization' (ibid., p. 104).

According to Freud the principal victims of these restrictions are women, whose social role is destined to be centred on the family and its affections, but who are unable to fulfil this function since men, by contrast, are expected to expend most of their time and energy working on behalf of the community. Innumerable prohibitions and restrictions are imposed on both sexes in the belief that sexuality is the same for all individuals, that is, heterosexual and monogamous; and in the refusal to admit that sexuality is a source of pleasure in its own right and not simply something to be tolerated for the purpose of propagating the species.

Society does not demand sacrifices only in terms of sexual satisfaction. The other natural human instinct, aggression, is also kept in check to suit the needs of society, and is only allowed to be directed against persons and groups foreign to the individual's particular social group, or towards a 'scapegoat' who will be used to syphen off this indomitable aggression: 'In circumstances that are favourable to it, when the mental counter-forces which ordinarily inhibit it are out of action, it also manifests itself spontaneously and reveals man as a savage beast to whom consideration towards his own kind is something alien' (ibid., pp. 111–12).

Civilized society is continually threatened with destruction because of this aggressive tendency. Even if we were able to establish a different social order, if we achieved total sexual freedom and abolished the family and the restrictions it imposes, 'one thing we can expect, and that is that this indestructible feature of human nature will follow it there' (ibid., p. 114). On the subject of happiness, Freud thinks that it is highly unlikely that a wholly satisfactory balance can be struck between the expectations of the individual and those of society. He acknowledges that people have a 'legitimate right' to revolt against a given social order in order to try to make it meet their requirements better, but the result will always fail to reconcile individual and collective needs, and this is the price we must pay for the security that civilization affords us by protecting us from the unrestrained satisfaction of our instincts which would inevitably lead to our downfall.

Freud's image of man

When Freud defines *civilization* he does so in terms of the ideals and, to some extent, the achievements of his epoch: a society may be considered to be civilized when it has succeeded in mastering the earth in order to protect man from the forces of nature and provide him, through developments in science and technology, with hitherto unsuspected means of advancing and increasing his control over nature and himself. To be civilized a society must also cultivate man's appreciation of beauty wherever he finds it, in nature as well as in art. It must promote cleanliness and order too, the first to encourage self-respect, the second to enable man to use space and time to his best advantage, thus preserving his psychic energy. Civilized society is also distinguished by the way in which it regulates the relationships between individuals according to tenets of justice which are equally applicable to all citizens, regardless of class, race, or rank. Individual freedom must be limited to meet the requirements of justice, and a craving for freedom can only be tolerated as a reaction to injustice within the community, not to society itself, since by its very nature society opposes the unconditional freedom of the individual.

Happiness, seen as the total satisfaction of our desires, and personal freedom must therefore be sacrificed in the interests of the progress of civilization which on the other hand guarantees our security. As Marcuse wrote in *Eros and*

Civilization, the concept of man that emerges from Freud's philosophy is at one and the same time the most irrefutable condemnation of Western civilization and its firmest defence.

Notably missing from Freud's theory is a concept which carries so much weight today: that technical and scientific progress may not be unlimited and might even have fatal consequences if rapacious and uncontrolled development is allowed to deprive society of the very advantages which were its original purpose. Freud is blissfully unaware of the possibility of a slump in energy resources, of environmental pollution and of the monstrous growth of industrialization which has deprived our lives of order, cleanliness and beauty. The social pessimism in his writings has no bearing on his typically nineteenth-century respect for progress.

Nor does he consider the extent to which a specific organization at a specific time can have a repressive effect on an individual, creating areas of alienation, as in the case of men exploited in their work, or working in the interests of others at the expense of their own. (This would be the direction of Marxist inquiry.) Freud's attention is clinically focused on what happens to a given individual within a given society, that of the Habsburgs in the late nineteenth century.

On the other hand, although Freud was not interested in politics in a narrow sense, as we have already seen, he was none the less firmly convinced that during the socializing process which the individual experiences within a family modelled on a given type of society, tensions and problems develop which make it increasingly hard for the individual (who unconsciously carries these conflicts in him) to cope with life and with his own alienation which prevents him from realizing his potential and achieving his personal free-dom. We therefore find in Freud the same 'social pessimism' as that expressed by the novelists of his day, the same lucid, implacable denunciation of the crippling effect of society on the individual, and the same bitter (or realistic) awareness of

the inevitable sacrifice of his natural inclinations that man has
to make in the interests of civilization. Yet the self-destructive
nihilism of Roth's works was foreign to him, as was the
descriptive approach of Schnitzler and the aristocratic detachment of Musil, whose hero in *The Man Without Qualities*
comes to terms with himself by alienating himself from the
outside world with its false beliefs and false consciousness.

The image of man that emerges from Freud's work is that
of an individual who strives to achieve what freedom he can,
within limits which are *external,* in that they are universal
(the demand of the collective) and *specific* to a particular form
of civilization. In Freud's time these specific limits were born
of the conflict between the values of a decadent society which
could no longer maintain them, and the eruption of individual
impulse, repressed or misunderstood, according to what is
known as the 'Victorian' ethic. Freud was well aware of this
conflict, and experienced it himself at its most dramatic. His
research helped the individual to achieve this freedom
through a new kind of self-awareness which extended the
reasoning process beyond conventional limits into the unexplored territory of the unconscious.

It has mistakenly been asserted that Freud invoked the
unconscious so as to exorcize it: as the exorcists of old drew
demons from those who were possessed in order to cure
them, so Freud was said to have neutralized the unconscious
mind with the powers of reason. In reality Freud had no wish
to subdue the instincts, only to integrate them in the overall
ego which was thus revived and enriched. In other words, the
aim of analysis is to make the ego 'master in its own house'.
This repossession of the part of the self which had been
alienated from consciousness occurs either when that which
was concealed in the most instinctual depths of the self is
revealed, or when the (equally unconscious) defences which
in the process of development have been responsible for a
pathological distortion of the ego are exposed.

This new 'self-awareness' is not so much a point of arrival, the definitive attainment of a rediscovered Truth which establishes itself immutably in the face of and beyond historical and personal development. Rather it should be seen as the ego's reacquired ability to assume a critical stance towards the inconsistencies and deceptions of reality as they appear within the individual. Throughout his life Freud was sustained by the hope of attaining this degree of self-awareness, just as much as by the constant revision of his analytical methods. He discovered a system which made the clinical analysis of his patients possible, which then served as a point of reference in understanding the human psyche. In the chapters which follow we shall examine Freud's progress from the early observations he made to the establishment of his own particular method.

Part II

Freud

3

The Two Sides of
Freud's Personality

The two sides of Freud (1)

On Easter Sunday, 25 April 1886, the following announcement appeared in the *Neue Freie Presse*, Vienna's most
authoritative and widely read daily paper: 'Dr Sigmund
Freud, lecturer in Neuropathology at the University of
Vienna, has returned from spending six months in Paris and
now resides at Rathausstrasse 7.' This announcement had
been inserted by Freud himself following his decision to set
up in private practice.

The Rathausstrasse was in the centre of Vienna where the
best medical practices were to be found. Freud's rented
surgery consisted of two good-sized rooms and a smaller
room reserved for ophthalmoscopy. It was furnished with
modest elegance, and had a number of shelves containing
Freud's well-stocked library, his only real possession.

Dr Sigmund Freud was one of the many Viennese prac-
titioners who set up on their own after numerous years of
research and infirmary work. He was no more and no less
famous than any of his colleagues, and his life-style and
habits were no different from theirs. He was a good-looking
man in his early thirties, of average height and build, with
dark hair, remarkably piercing dark eyes and a short, well-
trimmed beard. He dressed with meticulous attention to

detail but without ostentation, and his appearance suggested an order, dignity and conventionality typical of his class and standing. He was about to get married: in September 1886 he would be betrothed, according to Jewish custom, to Martha Bernays, the charming, well-educated daughter of an intellectual Jewish family. Freud, too, belonged to a Jewish family of Galician extraction which for financial reasons settled in Vienna in 1860 when Freud himself was four years old.

Like many other Jews the Freuds had come to Vienna from the neighbouring provinces, drawn by the lure of better commercial prospects, a higher standard of living and the liberal atmosphere prevailing there. In 1852 the severe restrictions imposed on the various Jewish communities scattered throughout the Empire had been lifted. Emancipation and the abolition of ghettos — which radically transformed the existence of many families, especially in the cities where they were more easily assimilated — produced an extraordinary surge of intellectual energy in the more intelligent and cultivated individuals. Joseph Breuer, a noted surgeon who was Freud's friend and protector during the years when he was struggling to establish himself, describes his own father, Leopold Breuer, as a man of that generation of Jews who first emerged from the constriction of the ghetto into the open air of the Western world. According to Breuer it was impossible for other people fully to appreciate the spiritual revival that that generation experienced when they were suddenly able to abandon their jargon for correct German and the restrictions of the ghetto for the civilized conditions of the Western world, and to gain access to the whole range of German literature, poetry and philosophy.

However, even in those wholly assimilated families who had completely abandoned the religion of their fathers, there survived the typically Jewish patriarchal concept of the family which consisted of an unshakeable faith in male supremacy and in the subordination of women, a respect for authority, for a sense of duty and hard work and a puritanical aversion to any kind of excess.

Freud had inherited all these characteristics, despite the fact that he had not been brought up as an orthodox Jew and was not religious by inclination. His everyday life was subjected to two different influences, therefore: on the one hand, the Austrian bourgeois tradition of the lower and middle classes, and on the other, the patriarchal and authoritative austerity of orthodox Jewish tradition.

Jakob Freud, Sigmund's father, was a woolmerchant who had never been particularly successful as a businessman but had managed to keep his family in reasonable comfort. None of the children had had their education curtailed; there was always enough money to buy books, theatre tickets and a piano; to pay for music lessons, a portrait of Sigmund at the age of nine and one of all the children some years later; for the acquisition of a modern, improved oil-lamp, the first of this kind in Vienna; besides which the family habitually spent their summer holidays at a Moravian resort. After his father's death Freud describes him in a letter to Fliess dated 2 November 1896 as a much-loved and respected parent whose profound wisdom and marvellous light-heartedness had had a great influence on him.

His mother, Amalia Nathanson, was Jakob's third wife. She was the daughter of a Viennese commercial agent, and was 20 when she gave birth to Sigmund, her first child, on 6 May 1856. All accounts of her agree that she was very beautiful but austere and authoritative, and that she deeply admired and trusted her eldest son.

The household included two of Freud's half-brothers from Jakob's first marriage who were about the same age as their stepmother. In the course of ten years six more children were born. The large patriarchal family was united by strong bonds of affection and governed by a traditional hierarchy. Sigmund was a loving and respectful son and as Amalia's eldest and favourite child he enjoyed certain privileges and prerogatives almost by right: a room of his own and the use of the only oil-lamp the family possessed. Respect for his peace and quiet was such that his sister Anne had to give up her piano lessons so as not to disturb his schoolboy concentration.

Throughout his primary and secondary education Freud was an alert and gifted pupil. During his eight years at grammar school he was six times top of his class, and he matriculated at the age of 17 *summa cum laude*. He enrolled at the School of Medicine in 1873 and graduated in 1881. Freud himself attributed this long lapse of time to his early liking for research: 'the habit of research, to which I have sacrificed a good deal, dissatisfaction with what the student is offered, the need to go into detail and exercise the critical faculty, are obstacles to the study of text-books' (*The Origins of Psycho-Analysis*, p. 57).

During these years he did some brilliant and scientifically precise research in zoology and physiology under the guidance of Brücke, and published his first articles, which won the approval of his mentors. A brilliant academic career was open to him, but his engagement to Martha Bernays in 1882 and the need to support a young family made him abandon pure research. Also in 1882 he began work at the General Hospital in Vienna, dedicating most of his time to his ward patients and to acquiring practical experience. However, he did not entirely give up research: he wrote articles on cerebral anatomy and clinical studies based on his observation of neurological patients which earned him the approval of his teacher, the psychiatrist Meynert, and of the prominent neurologists of the time. An official report on his professional qualifications as a medical officer during his military service in 1886 describes him as reliable and serious-minded, conscientious in his work, disciplined and trustworthy on duty, and obedient, frank and modest with his superiors. His general conduct was said to be very correct and unassuming.

Freud's five-year engagement to Martha was a very important period in his life. During this time they were often separated but this only strengthened their relationship which was sustained by a passionate but highly respectful correspondence. Terms of endearment are restricted almost entirely to the opening paragraph of Freud's letters, where he addresses his fiancée as his 'sweet, passionately loved child', 'Highness', 'dear love', 'little princess', 'blessed treasure'. Overtly erotic terms are few and far between. In one letter he asks to be forgiven for comparing his beloved's tiny feet to the Venus de Milo's much larger ones. In another he asks once again to be forgiven for having referred to an occasion when, while they were strolling with his sister Minna in the Beethovengang, Martha withdrew to pull up her stockings. In yet another he refuses to allow Martha to skate in case his beloved treasure should lean on another man's arm.

The long-awaited marriage was repeatedly postponed through respect for bourgeois convention: the young doctor, setting out on a career that offered little security and a great many risks, was overcome by scruples as to whether he could adequately support a wife.

In a long letter to Martha dated June 1882 he admits to a sense of inferiority because he is neither as handsome, rich, distinguished nor influential as his friend Ernst von Fleischl and because he is unable to give his beloved jewel a worthy setting; at times in the course of their correspondence, he sees science itself as a serious threat to his personal comfort which he describes to Martha in the following terms:

> All we need is two or three little rooms where we can live and eat and receive a guest and a hearth where the fire for cooking does not go out. And what things there will have to be: tables and chairs, beds, a mirror, a clock to remind the happy ones of the passage of time, an armchair for an hour of agreeable day-

dreaming, carpets so that the *Hausfrau* can easily keep the floor clean, linen tied up in fancy ribbons and stored on their shelves, clothes of the newest cut and hats with artificial flowers, pictures on the wall, glasses for the daily water and for wine on festive occasions, plates and dishes, a larder for when we are suddenly overcome with hunger or a guest arrives unexpectedly, a large bunch of keys which must rattle noisily. There is so much we can enjoy: the bookcase and the sewing basket and the friendly lamp. And everything must be kept in good order, else the *Hausfrau*, who has divided up her heart in little bits, one for each piece of furniture, will object. And this thing must be a witness to the serious work that keeps the house together, and that thing of one's love for beauty, of dear friends of whom one is glad to be reminded, of towns one has seen, of hours one likes to recall. All of it a little world of happiness, of silent friends and emblems of honourable humanity. (Quoted in Jones, *The Life and Works of Sigmund Freud*, pp. 138—9)

An idyllic vision, certainly, but very human and down to earth as well. Yet even such legitimate aspirations require money. Freud's lack of money is an irksome topic that underlies his entire correspondence with Martha and reaches a climax as the date of their wedding approaches. Jones, Freud's most reliable biographer, cites one of the most dramatic incidents in the couple's relationships: a quarrel between Freud and Martha's brother Eli which arose because Freud wrongly thought that Eli had invested some of her money unwisely.

Freud was sometimes annoyed by Martha's apparently unreasonable expectations about their future home, how they would furnish it, the rent they would pay, etc., although they were quite normal in a girl of that period: 'I have the impression that the dearest woman in the world is mortal on that point and regards a husband as a supplement — a necessary one, it is true — to a beautiful home' (ibid., p. 144).

He was indeed under pressure from all quarters, but mainly from his future mother-in-law, to make sure that the marriage would be financially viable:

> Don't think that I can't imagine how uncomfortable your present life is, but to run a household without the means for it is a *curse*. It is one I have myself borne for years, so I can judge. I beg and implore you not to do it. Do not let my warning go unheeded, and wait quietly until you have a settled means of existence.
>
> First regain some calmness and peace of mind which at present is so entirely wrecked. You have no reason whatever for your ill-humour and despondency, which borders on the pathological. Dismiss all these calculations, and first of all become once more a sensible *man*. At the moment you are like a spoilt *child* who can't get his own way and cries, in the belief that in that way he can get everything.
>
> Don't mind this last sentence but it is really true. Take to heart these truly well-meant words and don't think badly of
>
> > Your faithful
> > Mother
>
> > > (Ibid., p. 145)

It is clear from Freud's letters to his fiancée that his views on marriage and the mutual faithfulness and possessiveness of the married state are very conventional. We know also that he observed them throughout his married life. His attitude to the opposite sex is very clearly set down in a commentary on an essay by John Stuart Mill which he had translated in 1880. He starts by praising Mill for having succeeded better than anyone in freeing himself from the pressure of current prejudices. But at the same time he criticizes him for lacking a sense of the absurd, as for instance in a passage on the emancipation of women and on the subject of women in general. He goes on to say:

He had simply forgotten all that, like everything else concerning the relationship between the sexes. That is altogether a point with Mill where one simply cannot find him human. His autobiography is so prudish or so ethereal that one could never gather from it that human beings consist of men and women and that this distinction is the most significant one that exists. In his whole presentation it never emerges that women are different beings — we will not say lesser, rather the opposite — from men. He finds the suppression of women an analogy to that of Negroes. Any girl, even without a suffrage or legal competence, whose hand a man kisses and for whose love he is prepared to dare all, could have set him right. It is really a still-born thought to send women into the struggle for existence exactly as men. If, for instance, I imagined my gentle sweet girl as a competitor it would only end in my telling her, as I did seventeen months ago, that I am fond of her and that I implore her to withdraw from the strife into the calm uncompetitive activity of my home. It is possible that changes in upbringing may suppress all a woman's tender attributes, needful of protection and yet so victorious, and that she can then earn a livelihood like men. It is also possible that in such an event one would not be justified in mourning the passing away of the most delightful thing the world can offer — our ideal of womanhood. I believe that all reforming action in law and education would break down in front of the fact that, long before the age at which a man can earn a position in society, Nature has determined woman's destiny through beauty, charm, and sweetness. Law and custom have much to give women that has been withheld from them, but the position of women will surely be what it is: in youth an adored darling and in mature years a loved wife. (Ibid., p. 168)

The two sides of Freud (2)

All accounts concur to create an image of Freud as the traditional young Jewish doctor with a conservative middle

class background, eager to work hard for the sake of his
family as befits a responsible, loving husband and father. But
a more careful examination of the facts — based once again on
letters to his fiancée and to his friend Fliess — reveals a very
different picture. The placid scientist, the patient and conventional lover is in fact a man of violent, sometimes uncontrollable passions — or passions that are only controlled after a
painful inner (and not always inner) struggle. The slightest
suspicion of fickleness or neglect on the part of 'good, gentle
and generous Martha' casts a shadow of doubt over their
relationship, and his single-minded possessiveness, which
sometimes bordered on the absurd, put an intolerable strain
on Martha. Jones writes: 'Freud was evidently looking for
trouble, and he found it or made it. There was to be no other
male than himself in Martha's life, at all events in her
affection. This postulate seems also to have included her
mother' (ibid., p. 121). And again:

> Freud's attitude toward the loved one was very far from being
> one of simple attraction. It was a veritable *grande passion*. He
> was to experience in his own person the full force of the
> terrible power of love with all its raptures, fears and torments.
> It aroused all the passions of which his intense nature was
> capable. If ever a fiery apprenticeship qualified a man to
> discourse authoritatively on love that man was Freud. (Ibid.,
> p. 115)

Freud was not just trying to impress his fiancée. His
attitude was dictated by more painful if nobler feelings. He
yearned for a profound and total understanding with the one
he loved, but felt that he was unworthy of such good fortune.
He makes this clear in a letter written to Martha after an
outburst of violent, unjustified jealousy, which was provoked
by the presumed attentions of one of Martha's old friends:

Can there be anything crazier, I said to myself. You have won the dearest girl quite without any merit of your own, and you know no better than only a week later to reproach her with being tart and to torment her with jealousy . . . When a girl like Martha is fond of me how can I fear a Max Mayer or a legion of Max Mayers? . . . It was the expression of my clumsy, self-tormenting kind of deeply rooted love . . . Now I have shaken it off like a disease . . . The feeling I had about Max Mayer came from a distrust of myself, not of you. (Ibid., p. 116)

As well as being jealous Freud envied people who were more attractive than himself, who could captivate others with their charm in a way he was convinced that he could not; he was also furious that Martha was not prepared to give up her love for her mother, her admiration for Eli her brother, or the religious orthodoxy in which she had been brought up. But Jones maintains that Martha's solid good sense made Freud lose many an irrational battle, and that once reason again prevailed over his violent passions he was glad to have lost.

It is interesting to note that while being so emotionally embroiled in his relationship with Martha, he later wrote lucid attacks on the repressive, authoritarian conventions which then prevailed and which he held responsible for most of the psychic disturbances to which women are prone. I shall quote extensively from his essay ' "Civilized" Sexual Morality and Modern Nervous Illness' published in 1908, 22 years after his marriage.

Freud first examines a text by Ehrenfels, professor of philosophy at the University of Prague, in which he contrasts *natural* sexual morality (in which the human race remains strong and healthy) with *civilized* sexual morality (in the observation of which men are spurred on to work hard in the interests of social productivity). Freud maintains that civilized sexual morality is harmful since it represses people's sexual urges, and he asks whether civilized sexual morality is worth the sacrifice it involves, especially since our hedonistic inclinations still compel us to see personal satisfaction as one of the aims of cultural progress. If it is harmful to men, it is twice as harmful to women in a society where male transgressions are more readily tolerated and which thus applies a double standard that encourages its members to disguise reality and to deceive themselves and others.

It is clear that education is far from underestimating the task of suppressing a girl's sensuality till her marriage, for it makes use of the most drastic measures. Not only does it forbid sexual intercourse and set a high premium on the preservation of female chastity, but it also protects the young woman from temptation as she grows up, by keeping her ignorant of all the facts of the part she is to play and by not tolerating any impulse of love in her which cannot lead to marriage. The result is that when the girl's parental authorities suddenly allow her to fall in love, she is unequal to this psychical achievement and enters marriage uncertain of her own feelings. In consequence of this artificial retardation in her function of love, she has nothing but disappointments to offer the man who has saved up all his desire for her. In her mental feelings she is still attached to her parents, whose authority has brought about the suppression of her sexuality; and in her physical behaviour she shows herself frigid, which deprives the man of any high degree of sexual enjoyment. I do not know whether the anaesthetic type of woman exists apart from civilized education, though I consider it probable. But in any case such education actually breeds it, and these women who conceive without pleasure show little willingness afterwards to face the pains of frequent childbirth. In this way, the preparation for marriage frustrates the aims of marriage itself. When later on the retardation in the wife's development has been overcome and her capacity to love is awakened at the climax of her life as a woman, her relations to her husband have long since been ruined; and, as a reward for her previous docility, she is left with the choice between unappeased desire, unfaithfulness or a neurosis. (Standard edn, vol. IX, pp. 197–8)

Here we see clearly how Freud exploited the profound discrepancy between his emotions and his reason. Freud the future husband, was at odds with Freud the rational man who could objectively diagnose inconsistencies within society and within himself. As Jones observes: 'He was beyond doubt someone whose instincts were far more powerful than those of the average man, but whose repressions were even more potent. The combination brought about an inner intensity of a degree that is perhaps the essential feature of any great genius' (Jones, *The Life and Works of Sigmund Freud,* p. 136). It may be added that Freud's powers of reasoning drew on this very 'inner intensity' which resulted from the struggle between conflicting needs, a struggle he resolved with varying degrees of success over the years.

There is not a single trait of his character, nor a decision he made nor an incident in his life, that cannot be interpreted in two different ways. For instance, he repeatedly asserted that he was not ambitious, but just as often he contradicted this statement. Here is a passage from a letter that clearly expresses this inconsistency:

There was a time when I was only eager to learn and ambitious and grieved every day that Nature had not, in one of her gracious moods, imprinted on me the stamp of genius as she sometimes does. Since then I have long known that I am no genius, and I no longer understand how I could have wished to be one. I am not even very talented; my whole capacity for work probably lies in my character attributes and in the lack of any marked intellectual deficiency. But I know that that admixture is very favourable for slowly winning success, that under favourable conditions I could achieve more than Nothnagel, to whom I feel myself superior, and

that perhaps I might attain Charcot's level. That doesn't mean
that I shall, since I shan't find those favourable conditions and
I do not possess the genius or the force to compel them.
(Ibid., p. 183)

In fact since his very first research work as a student Freud
had been intent on achieving some sensational scientific
discovery — not to gain social or professional acclaim, but in
the interest of mankind in general. His self-confidence, which
he ascribed to his mother's strong affection and admiration
for her firstborn, was frequently shaken, but always reasser-
ted itself with as much tenacity and optimism as before.

> There is some courage and boldness locked up in me that is
> not easily driven away or extinguished. When I examine
> myself strictly, more strictly than my loved one would, I
> perceive that Nature has denied me many talents and has
> granted me not much, indeed very little, of the kind of talent
> that compels recognition. But she endowed me with a daunt-
> less love of truth, the keen eye of an investigator, a rightful
> sense of the values of life, and the gift of working hard and
> finding pleasure in doing so. Enough of the best attributes for
> me to find endurable my beggarliness in other respects . . . We
> will hold together through this life, so easily apprehensible in
> its immediate aims but so incomprehensible in its final
> purpose. (Ibid., p. 123)

He was, as we have seen, extremely punctilious in matters
of propriety, but at heart he was equally intolerant of such
restrictions, as he made clear to his future wife: 'Our life will
hardly be as idyllic as you paint it. Even if I become Docent,
lecturing will not come my way, and my Martha, a born
German Frau Professor, will have to do without her fine
position. Nor should I have been suited to it. I still have
something wild within me, which as yet has not found any
proper expression' (ibid., p. 183). As to the docile, dutiful

medical officer described in the report mentioned earlier, it is interesting to note his own reaction to the disconcerting bureaucracy and hierarchy of military life. Here, in a letter written in 1886 to his friend Breuer, he gives free rein to his caustic wit:

Here I am tied fast in this filthy hole — I can't think how else to describe it — and am working on black and yellow. I have been giving lectures on field hygiene: the lectures were pretty well attended and have even been translated into Czech. I have not yet been 'confined to barracks' . . . We play at war all the time — once we even carried out the siege of a fortress — and I play at being an army doctor, dealing out chits on which ghastly wounds are noted. While my battalion is attacking I lie down on some stony field with my men. There is fake ammunition as well as fake leadership, but yesterday the General rode past and called out 'Reserves, where would you be if they had used live ammunition? Not one of you would have escaped.'

The only bearable thing in Olmütz is a first-class café with ice, newspapers, and good confectionery. Like everything else the service there is affected by the military system. When two or three generals — I can't help it, but they always remind me of parakeets, for mammals don't usually dress in such colours (save for the back parts of baboons) — sit down together, the whole troop of waiters surround them and nobody else exists for them. Once in despair I had to have recourse to swank. I grabbed one of them by the coat-tails and shouted, 'Look here, I might be a general sometime, so fetch me a glass of water.' That worked.

An officer is a miserable creature. Each envies his colleagues, bullies his subordinates, and is afraid of his superiors; the higher up he is, the more he fears them. I detest the idea of having inscribed on my collar how much I am worth, as if I were a sample of some goods. And nevertheless the system has its gaps. The Commanding Officer was here recently from Brünn and went into the swimming-baths, when I was

astonished to observe that his trunks carried no marks of
distinction! (Ibid., pp. 180—1)

Freud came from a Jewish family and he remained a Jew.
None the less, he was intolerant of orthodox rites and
traditions and his friend Jones reveals that this was a cause of
friction between him and Martha. However, the fact that he
belonged to a minority sect began to preoccupy Freud from
1873 when he was at university at the very time at which he
became aware of anti-Semitic prejudice. Disturbed by the
realization that his Jewish origins placed him in a position of
unwarranted inferiority in relation to his colleagues, he
rebelled against this situation: 'These first impressions at the
University, however, had one consequence which was afterwards to prove important; for at an early age I was made
familiar with the fate of being in the Opposition and of being
put under the ban of the "compact majority". The foundations
were thus laid for a certain degree of independence of
judgement' (*An Autobiographical Study,* standard edn, vol.
XX, p. 9).

As a student his qualities were recognized by prominent
figures in the world of science and medicine, and especially in
his early years he seems to have felt a need for protection and
trust and to have been inclined to worship the 'revered
masters' with whom he collaborated in the laboratory or in
the hospital wards. His friendships were often intense and
very intimate — with Breuer as we have seen, and initially with
his near-contemporary, Fliess, the famous ear-nose-and-
throat specialist, for whom he developed a violent affection
and an unconditional admiration. His relationships tended to
follow a pattern, cooling down after a period of total amity
and ending in overt hostility. His friendship with and subsequent estrangement from Jung followed this pattern. Freud
was well aware of this trait in his character. With the rare
ability he had to be objective about himself, he related this

fiery rebellious streak in his nature to a very ambivalent childhood relationship, part admiring affection, part burning rivalry, which he had experienced with his nephew, the son of a half-brother, who was a year older than himself:

> Until the end of my third year we had been inseparable; we had loved each other and fought each other, and, as I have already hinted, this childhood relation has determined all my later feelings in my intercourse with persons of my own age. My nephew John has since then had many incarnations, which have revivified first one and then another aspect of a character that is ineradicably fixed in my unconscious memory. At times he must have treated me very badly, and I must have opposed my tyrant courageously . . . An intimate friend and a hated enemy have always been indispensable to my emotional life; I have always been able to create them anew, and not infrequently my childish ideal has been so closely approached that friend and enemy have coincided in the same person: but not simultaneously, of course, as was the case in my early childhood. (Jones, *The Life and Works of Sigmund Freud*, p. 37)

When he came to analyse his own dreams Freud also discovered the extent to which his equally ambivalent relationship with his father was responsible for his initially docile and submissive attitude towards his teachers, which invariably changed into one of hostile antagonism. This was a shock to him for he had considered himself to be a devoted son, and it proved to be a landmark in his scientific investigation of the unknown.

As we have said, Freud was an excellent and keen scholar, with a particular aptitude for ancient history and languages. At 20 he spoke fluent French, German, English and Spanish, and had read and enjoyed the classics — Homer, Cervantes and especially Shakespeare and Goethe — as well as a number of modern French and English novels. His German teachers praised the excellence of his German style. Yet in spite of his predominant interest in history and languages he opted for a career in medicine, although on various occasions he admitted that he felt no particular inclination towards that subject. What determined his choice?

There is no doubt that medicine was highly regarded in the cultural circles of *fin de siècle* Vienna, and medical progress seemed to match the progress of humanity itself. But Freud states that what decided him had nothing to do with the traditional view of medicine as medical practice or as research: 'Neither at that time, nor indeed in my later life, did I feel any particulr predilection for the career of a doctor. I was moved, rather, by a sort of curiosity, which was, however, directed more towards human concerns than towards natural objects; nor had I grasped the importance of observation as one of the best means of gratifying it' (*An Autobiographical Study*, standard edn, vol. XX, p. 8). According to Freud, what made him decide to enrol in the School of Medicine was a public lecture by Carl Brühl on Goethe's essay *On Nature*, which depicts nature as a generous and beautiful mother who *allows her children to explore her secrets*. So a great poet was responsible for directing Freud's steps towards science, albeit a peculiar science, probing beyond the boundaries of observed reality into areas which are more usually the preserve of poets and novelists. In a letter to Martha dated 16 July 1882 Freud describes the violent impression made on him by Flaubert's *Les tentations de St Antoine*, and once again it is evident that the unexplored and perhaps unexplorable holds great fascination for him:

> and now on top of it all came this book which in the most condensed fashion and with unsurpassable vividness throws at one's head the whole trashy world: for it calls up not only the great problems of knowledge, but the real riddles of life, all the conflicts of feelings and impulses; and it confirms the

awareness of our perplexity in the mysteriousness that reigns everywhere. These questions, it is true, are always there, and one should always be thinking of them . . . but they suddenly assail one in the morning and rob one of one's composure and one's spirits. (Jones, *The Life and Works of Sigmund Freud*, p. 167)

Freud's was a form of science akin to great poetry and literature in its purpose, yet distinct from them in the systematic and objective way it relied on experimentation, using a precise logic, not just to present facts but to systematize them into blueprints that might enable us to 'penetrate the enigma'. Freud confirms that in his early years his main aspirations were philosophical: 'In my youth I felt an overpowering need to understand something of the riddles of the world in which we live and perhaps even to contribute something to their solution' (ibid., p. 54). And in a letter to Fliess dated 1 January 1896: 'I see that you are using the circuitous route of medicine to attain your first ideal, the physiological understanding of man, while I secretly nurse the hope of arriving by the same route at my own original objective, philosophy. For that was my original ambition, before I knew what I was intended to do in the world' (*The Origins of Psycho-Analysis*, p. 141).

Yet Freud was far from uncritical of philosophy, and many years later, in 1932, he explained the reasons for his disenchantment. In the thirty-fifth lecture of his *Introductory Lectures on Psycho-Analysis*, replying to the question of whether psychoanalysis is conducive to a given *Weltanschauung*, or concept of the world, and if so, to which, Freud defines *Weltanschauung* as 'an intellectual construction which solves all the problems of our existence uniformly on the basis of one overriding hypothesis, which, accordingly, leaves no question unanswered and in which everything that interests us finds its fixed place' (*New Introductory Lectures on Psycho-Analysis,* standard edn, vol. XXII, p. 158). This philosophical objective can only be an illusion, vulnerable to every advance in our understanding of human nature. In rejecting it, Freud added that he had found some justification for Heine's definition of the philosopher as one who patches up the universe with bits and pieces.

While admitting that philosophy is an expression of man's loftier aspirations and that faith in it may help us to know what to expect of life and how to make the most of our affections and interests, Freud declares that psychoanalysis is totally unfit to create its own *Weltanschauung* and must accept that which science itself has to offer. 'It asserts that there are no sources of knowledge of the universe other than the intellectual working-over of carefully scrutinized observations — in other words, what we call research' (ibid., p. 159). And this research is continually evolving, quick to retrace the paths of its own certainties whenever these prove to be illusory or wrong; 'he is not all-embracing, he has no pretensions to be all-fulfilling, or to providing a system'.

We shall see later how Freud's working method always adheres to this critical approach, even towards his own findings, and how his reasoning, straining to throw light on what is not well known, refers beyond the illuminated circle of knowledge to a new zone of shadow waiting to be explored in a process which is interminable.

The way in which Freud developed and cross-fertilized his interest in literature, philosophy and science in the early years typified the unique approach of the future founder of the science of psychoanalysis. He himself described his mental attitude as follows:

> You often estimate me too highly. For I am not really a man of science, not an observer, not an experimenter, and not a thinker. I am nothing but by temperament a *conquistador* — an adventurer, if you want to translate the word — with the

curiosity, the boldness and the tenacity that belong to that type of being. Such people are apt to be treasured if they succeed, if they have really discovered something; otherwise they are thrown aside. And that is not altogether unjust. (Quoted in Jones, *The Life and Works of Sigmund Freud*, p. 297)

It is therefore not surprising that this *conquistador* failed to find true satisfaction in chemical or zoological research or, later, in physiological research in Brücke's laboratory or in research into cerebral anatomy under Meynert, although he took pride in his achievements, as is shown in a letter to Martha dated February 1884:

I really do wish you had been present to hear my lecture today, Marty. I haven't had such a triumph for a long time. Just imagine your timid lover, confronted by the severe Meynert and an assembly of psychiatrists and several colleagues, trying to draw attention to one of his earlier works, the very one which had been overlooked by Prof. Kupfer. Imagine him beginning with allusions, unable to control his voice, then drawing on the blackboard, in the middle of it all managing to make a joke at which the audience bursts out laughing! The moments in which he is afraid of getting stuck, each time fortunately concealed, become fewer, he slides into the waters of discussion where he sails about for a full hour, then Meynert with some words of praise expresses the assembly's vote of thanks, follows this up with a few appreciative observations then dissolves the meeting and shakes him by the hand. Then the old gentlemen who hitherto had ignored him congratulate him and gather round him to make a few belated comments . . . at last he leaves in an elated mood, wondering whether his work won't after all succeed in making his girl his own. Oh, but now comes the worry about holding one's own, finding something new to make the world sit up and bring not only recognition from the few but also attract the many, the well-paying public. (*Letters*, p. 114)

Freud's need to assert himself — which was part *con-quistador's* daring and curiosity, part scientific tenacity and part the more down-to-earth but no less urgent preoccupation of a prospective young husband — compelled him to seek some area of personal research the results of which would attract public attention. Two pieces of work seemed as if they might fulfil this aim. In the first instance he devised a method to assist neurological research by dyeing the nervous tissues with gold chloride, but although it won much praise, this method proved too costly to be practical. Secondly, he discovered the analgesic properties of cocaine, an alkaloid whose effects were little known in those days. Freud there-fore deduced that it might have anaesthetic properties also, and might be useful in surgery. But the ophthalmologist Carl Koller was the first to make systematic experiments with the drug, and it was he who became famous and successful as a result.

Freud's obsession with the desire to make a discovery of universal significance had consequences which proved damaging to his career. He had experimented on himself with cocaine without ill effect, and decided, being completely ignorant of the dangerous nature of the drug, to prescribe it to his very dear friend Fleischl-Marxow who was suffering from morphia poisoning, as a result of taking morphia to relieve unbearable neuralgia. The unexpected result was cocaine poisoning: Fleischl-Marxow's protracted agony was punc-tuated by fits of excruciating pain for which ever-stronger doses of cocaine were prescribed until death finally released him. Freud's faith in the curative properties of the drug thus proved fatal. When cases of cocaine addiction began to spread through Europe, and to be diagnosed, he faced justifiably bitter criticism.

His prospects as a young neurologist on the threshold of marriage were thus far from rosy, but fortunately he was regarded as an outstanding research student by his professors, and thanks to the backing of Brücke and Meynert he obtained a university post as a neuropathologist in April 1885, and was thus able to practise his profession with a certain authority, charge higher fees and establish his reputation to a certain extent. The situation improved when Freud was given a grant which enabled him to go to Paris from autumn 1885 to spring 1886 to study under the great neurologist Charcot, then at the peak of his career. Following in the steps of Charcot, Freud discovered the psychological element in neurology, and from then on psychology became his dominant interest and the subject of his own original work.

We now know Doctor Freud a little better: an austere and reserved-looking man, whose behaviour is characterized by the most rigorous respect for the conservative customs of his time, who conceals an unconventional, rebellious, impassioned and indomitable nature; an attentive and methodical scientist who uses scientific discipline to hold in check an imaginative and speculative nature continually straining towards new hypotheses which enable light to be thrown on the world's enigmas; a philosopher and scientist intolerant of philosophy and science where these manifest themselves as closed systems dogmatically anchored to their own certitudes. If, as he himself says, 'membership of the Jewish race pushed him from the beginning into the ranks of the opposition and ostracism from the solid majority'; if there was certainly present in him an awareness of his own contradictions, between a prudent and judicious adherence to the ideological scheme of things in his day and an extremely lucid rationality straining to demystify them, it is no accident that from such a personality should be born a psychology the central theme of which is conflict.

It is the same conflict of the historic moment which reverberates in Freud with redoubled intensity, fed, as Jones says, 'by far more powerful impulses than [those of] the average man, and ever more forceful repressions'. Freud's scientific work, sustained by his many-sided intelligence which embraced a variety of interests and a relentless desire for knowledge, reached unusual heights precisely because it was nourished by this tension between contrasting inner values. Dominated by reasoning powers aware of the contradictory nature of reality and the form which this reality takes in the individual, unbeknown to him, Freud's rationality strained to demystify the *known* and embrace that which in *unknown* ways throws into confusion everyday habits, certainties and beliefs.

Chronology

1856 Sigmund Freud is born in Freiberg, Moravia, on 6 May.

1860 The family moves to Vienna because of financial difficulties.

1873 At the end of a successful school career Freud passes his school-leaving examination with flying colours.

1874 He enrols at the School of Medicine. Alongside his university studies he carries out his own research work in neurology under Brücke, and in psychology under Meynert. His interest is focused on the neurological aspect of psychology.

1881 He passes his final examinations in medicine.

1882 He meets Martha Bernays and they become engaged on 17 June. On Brücke's advice he gives up pure research — which in financial terms also offered little security. He starts work at the General Hospital in Vienna where he remains until August 1885. In September his friend Breuer tells him about the case of Anna O. whom he has treated by hypnosis.

1884   He publishes a monograph on cocaine.

1885   Backed by his teachers and the foremost neurologists of the day Freud is given the post of lecturer in neuropathology at the University of Vienna on 3 September.

1886   Freud decides to use a grant he has received from the Faculty of Medicine to attend Charcot's courses in Paris (October 1885 — February 1886). On Easter Sunday he sets up his own surgery. In September he marries Martha Bernays.

4

Beginnings

Freud and Charcot

Freud's meeting with Charcot in 1885 proved crucial. What had driven him to use the grant he had been awarded to go to the Salpêtrière clinic and study under Charcot? Was it Charcot's scientific prestige, his research methods, or the personality of the famous physician? Charcot certainly shared many of Freud's characteristics and qualities: he was energetic and strong-minded; he had a sound scientific grounding in the field of pathological anatomy, a voracious appetite for knowledge and a scientific approach based on continual reassessment of observations made on the inmates of the Salpêtrière combined with a lucid theoretical analysis of the data thus acquired. Like Freud he was a very cultured man. He knew a great deal about the history of art and was a brilliantly lucid writer. He spoke fluent English, German and Italian and could quote Dante and Shakespeare in the original. He had other achievements to which Freud no doubt aspired: unquestioned scientific prestige, undisputed authority in the school he had founded at the Salpêtrière and an impressive professional position. He was known to be the private physician of kings and princes, and of various famous and influential people. Charcot had become very wealthy as a result of the fees he charged his exceptionally well-to-do patients, and his wife was wealthy in her own right. He therefore enjoyed a very high standard of living. He had a magnificent house and open access to the kind of society immortalized by Marcel Proust in *A la recherche du temps perdu*. Lavish receptions attended by scientists, politicians, artists and writers were held every Tuesday in his residence on the Boulevard Saint Germain, which was furnished like a museum with Renaissance works of art, rare books, stained glass windows, carpets and signed portraits.

This aspect of Charcot's life, which was in total contrast to Freud's austere withdrawn nature, can hardly have contributed to the great master's impact on the young Viennese neurologist. But Freud was irresistibly attracted by Charcot's interest in hysteria and hypnosis, particularly since it was rare for a physician of his standing to study these two subjects which were generally disregarded by official medicine.

It is common knowledge that when, in 1882, Charcot read his essay on 'Different Nervous Conditions Diagnosed by Means of Hypnosis' to the Académie des Sciences in Paris, he had the greatest difficulty in inducing its members to accept the validity of hypnosis, which under the name of *magnetism* they had already rejected three times in the course of the previous century. Thus once again it is Charcot's defiant attitude to research which attracted Freud, as did his desire to win over to reason and science a process that was still obscure and controversial, practised alike by doctors and charlatans, by faith-healers and academics, by socialites and by qualified therapists.

When Freud arrived in Paris in 1885 Charcot was delivering a series of lectures on 'Traumatic Paralyses' at the Salpêtrière before a vast and eclectic audience. Paralyses were termed 'traumatic' when they occurred in either male or female patients who had no lesions of the nervous system but presented the same symptoms as organically injured patients:

contractures, paralysis of an arm or a leg or some other part of the body, numbness, etc. A similar phenomenon occurred in the hysterics whom Charcot had treated in previous years. What caused these symptoms? According to current opinion they were mainly due, in the case of hysteria, either to simulation (hence the lack of medical interest in the condition) or, where women were concerned, to some genital disorder. Indeed hysteria, which is in fact more common among women than men, was considered to be a specifically female complaint. However, Charcot diagnosed cases of traumatic paralysis in three male patients at the Salpêtrière who suffered from partial paralysis of one arm as a result of psychic traumas, and he was able to prove that such symptoms were identical to those of hysterical paralysis. He was also able to induce these same symptoms artificially under hypnosis (by suggesting to the hypnotized patient that his arm was paralysed). He then demonstrated that the paralysis thus induced could be gradually dispelled by suggestion.

He also experimented with post-hypnotic suggestion, that is, he would suggest to a patient under hypnosis that when he emerged from his trance his arm would become paralysed at a given signal, and this invariably happened.

Charcot classified hysterical paralyses, both post-traumatic and hypnotic, under the single heading of *non-organic* phenomena, or phenomena that were not caused by some lesion in the main nervous system, but by a *specifically psychological factor* producing exactly the same symptoms as an organic lesion.

This was Charcot's main contribution to Freud's scientific education. In addition to this important practical element, Charcot's mental attitude reinforced Freud's own opinion that the scientist must have the courage to take into consideration even the most unexpected data yielded by an experiment, and must use them in a dynamic way to further theoretical research:

Many of Charcot's demonstrations began by provoking in me and in other visitors a sense of astonishment and an inclination to scepticism, which we tried to justify by an appeal to one of the theories of the day. He was always friendly and patient in dealing with such doubts, but he was always most decided; it was in one of these discussions that (speaking of theory) he remarked '*Ca n'empêche pas d'exister*', a *mot* which left an indelible mark upon my mind. (*An Autobiographical Study*, standard edn, vol. XX, p. 13)

A digression

We have seen that although hypnotism was already widely practised in lay circles when Charcot delivered his 1882 lecture before the Académie des Sciences it was not readily accepted as a scientific method. Why was scientific officialdom so grudging towards and suspicious of a method whose positive merits had been demonstrated? Was not hypnotism, although not recognized in official circles, one of the nineteenth century's medical discoveries?

In *The Discovery of the Unconscious*, to which we refer the reader for a more thoroughly documented account, Ellenberger suggests that the practice of scientific psychiatry which tries to explain and cure pathological psychic phenomena by investigating and exploiting individual or group psychology can be traced back to prehistoric times, and that the discoveries and theories of the great nineteenth-century psychologists relate back to these. Ellenberger also notes an interesting link between primitive medicine and exorcism, exorcism and mesmerism, and mesmerism and hypnosis, and even detects a socio-political element at the basis of these therapeutic systems which may account for their finding favour and subsequently falling into disrepute. We give here a brief outline of their history.

According to Ellenberger, the foundations of 'dynamic psychiatry' were laid when the methods used by the priest and exorcist Gassner were superseded by those of Dr Mesmer, the originator of mesmerism, in 1775. The new illuminism, with its unconditional faith in reason and its total rebuttal of mystical and irrational forces, caused Gassner's fall from power. Gassner was an exorcist, that is, he was able to cure what he called preternatural afflictions which are either the work of the devil — who causes the patient to experience symptoms similar to those of natural diseases — or of witchcraft, or the result of demonic possession (when the demon actually inhabits the patient's body). Ellenberger quotes an eyewitness account of one of Gassner's healing sessions. His first two patients were nuns who had been expelled from their religious communities because they were subject to convulsions. Gassner apparently made the first one kneel in front of him, then asked her her name, what was the matter with her and whether she would do as he told her. When she had agreed to do so he solemnly pronounced the following words in Latin: 'If there is anything preternatural in this patient I order that, in the name of Jesus Christ, it should manifest itself at once.' The patient immediately had a convulsive fit, thus proving, according to Gassner, that she was possessed by an evil spirit and not the victim of some natural disorder. He then proceeded to the second stage, commanding the evil spirit, still in Latin, to produce convulsions in various parts of the patient's body, and he asked the patient to appear as if she was in pain, then as if she was stupid, obsessed, angry, etc., even dead. His commands were carried out exactly and the demon was apparently overcome, so its actual expulsion from the patient's body was relatively easy. Gassner then turned to the second nun and repeated the process. After the session was over a certain Abbé Bourgeois asked one of the women if she had been in great pain, and she replied that she had only the vaguest memory of what had happened, but she did not think she had been in pain. Gassner then treated a third patient, a well-born lady who suffered from depression. He succeeded in exorcizing her depression and told her what she should do if it recurred.

Gassner was not merely tolerated by the Catholic church; exorcism was held by it to be a normal, salutary activity as long as it was practised with moderation and in strict compliance with Roman ritual: the patient had to declare his absolute faith in Jesus Christ and his earnest desire to be rid of the evil spirit.

Mesmer, on the other hand, was a physician and as a confirmed illuminist he opposed a method that was so popular among so-called mystics and faith-healers; but the assumptions on which his theory were based appear to us no less irrational than those of what he called Gassner's 'witchcraft'. However, in the eyes of his contemporaries, for the most part worshippers at the altar of science who had not yet mastered the basics of the new learning, his assumptions seemed more amenable to reason than did the other's miraculous healings.

Mesmer's theory was that (1) a tenuous natural fluid fills the universe and links man to the earth, the heavenly bodies and even to other men; (2) illnesses are caused by a non-homogeneous distribution of this fluid within the human body; they are cured by restoring the balance; (3) using certain methods the fluid can be channelled, stored and transmitted to other people; (4) in this way it is possible to provoke 'attacks' and thus cure the disease.

Mesmer called this fluid 'animal magnetism'. He would transmit it to the patient by standing in front of him and looking into his eyes while establishing some point of physical contact. He would then pass his hand gently over the body of the patient who immediately had an attack, and after repeated attacks the illness was gradually overcome.

He also performed collective cures in which up to 200

people participated. In these cases the magnetic fluid was transmitted by means of a basin of magnetized water known as the *baquet* which was linked to patients by means of metal tubes. It was always the presence of Mesmer himself which provoked the healing attacks. Such attacks were both *diagnosis* (in that they proved that the patient suffered from a magnetic disease) and *cure*. The poorer patients, peasants who lived in the country, for instance, gathered in a circle round a tree which served as a magnetic element. But it was always necessary for Mesmer to be present and to transmit his own animal magnetism in order that the attacks might occur in those who were predisposed to them. Those who did not respond to this treatment were sent to traditional doctors.

Both Mesmer and Gassner before him were worldwide celebrities and although Gassner always treated patients free of charge, Mesmer amassed a vast fortune, thus attracting the envy of others and fuelling the not unjustified suspicions of medical officialdom. The decline in Mesmer's popularity was due to a notable decrease in his mysterious power during the last years of his life, culminating in a resounding failure when he was summoned by Frederick II's brother Prince Henry II of Prussia to give a demonstration of his method.

He was succeeded by one of his most devoted disciples, the Marquis Puységur (1751–1825) who, according to Charcot's pupil and collaborator at the Salpêtrière, Charles Riquet, was the true founder of mesmerism. Puységur practised mesmerism in a philanthropic fashion on his own peasants when they were sick. His personal contribution to magnetism was the discovery that when mesmerized, some patients did not experience attacks but instead fell into a strange sleep, becoming more alert and receptive than before and demonstrating a livelier intelligence than usual. During these trances they were able to diagnose their own illness or that of other patients participating in the experiment, and after they had woken up they could carry out orders that had been given to them while they were asleep.

Obviously we are here on the threshold of hypnotism. The essential factors linking these experiments with the dynamic psychology that was to follow are:

The knowledge that certain pathological symptoms are due to psychic and not organic factors even when they appear to be similar to those organically provoked.

The symptoms are treated by psychic methods rather than by traditional methods such as pharmacology or surgery.

The person responsible for this treatment has a particular hold over the social group, because he possesses exceptional powers (like Gassner) or scientific authority (like Mesmer) or social standing (the Marquis Puységur was a member of one of the most influential and respected families of the French aristocracy).

An intense relationship is established between the patient and the healer based on their shared belief (Christian faith in the case of Gassner, faith in animal magnetism in that of Mesmer and Puységur).

According to Ellenberger (*The Discovery of the Unconscious*), despite numerous experiments and the genuine recovery of many patients, the integrity of the exponents of these methods of healing was persistently refuted by the Académie des Sciences for a variety of reasons throughout the nineteenth century. Instead of concentrating on the study of the more elementary manifestations of hypnotic trance, most mesmerists thought that the more sensational aspects of their method would prove its validity. Most lacked professional qualifications, and on the whole they chose to put ignorant and impressionable people into a trance and then asked them to diagnose illnesses and prescribe cures. To all intents and purposes this was an extremely illegal form of medical practice which aroused the anger of the professional physicians. There were also gangs of charlatans who exploited mesmerism as a very profitable side-show, sometimes provoking attacks of collective madness, and one way and another giving mesmerism a very bad name.

Between 1860 and 1880 mesmerism and hypnotism fell into total disrepute. Then Dr Ambroise Liébeault revived the methods and practised them in his own surgery at Nancy in Lorraine; and Bernheim of Alsace followed Liébeault's initiative and developed a structured theory of the subject. Bernheim, who held the chair of medicine at the University of Nancy, adopted Liébeault's hypnotic method in 1882, shortly after Charcot had given his famous lecture on hypnosis, and in 1886 he published his own article on the subject, in which he disagreed with Charcot. We shall see later in what respects the two schools — the school of Nancy whose experiments and theories were initiated by Liébeault, and Charcot's French school — held different views.

Freud and hypnosis

Let us now return to Freud. Even before his visit to Charcot Freud was interested in hypnosis. He describes how he first came across hypnosis in an unscientific context when he was still a student. We have seen how hypnotism developed at a tangent to official science during the nineteenth century, and was viewed with alternating interest and derision. However, theatrical performances featuring professional mesmerists or hypnotists of European fame did not fail to attract young neurologists and scientists who were intrigued by their peculiar experiments. Freud's own curiosity was aroused by a hypnotist named Hansen who drew vast crowds whenever he demonstrated his technique in Austria or Germany.

> While I was still a student I attended a public exhibition given by the 'magnetist' Hansen and had noticed that one of the persons experimented upon had become deathly pale at the onset of cataleptic rigidity and had remained so as long as the condition lasted. This firmly convinced me of the genuineness of the phenomena of hypnosis . . . And now the news reached us that a school had arisen at Nancy which made an extensive and remarkably successful use of suggestion, with or without hypnosis, for therapeutic purposes. It thus came about, as a matter of course, that in the first years of my activity as a physician my principal instrument of work, apart from haphazard and unsystematic psychotherapeutic methods, was hypnotic suggestion. (*An Autobiographical Study*, standard edn, vol. XX, pp. 16—17)

It is interesting that Freud the scientist should declare that the origin of his interest in hypnotism was a theatre performance because it throws light on the way Freud's mind worked. In accordance with positivist science he was interested in facts as they were presented to him in their undeniable reality and certainty. However, among these facts he was particularly interested in the singularity of a phenomenon and the degree to which it could not be explained according to the 'clear and distinct' theories and laws hitherto established by science.

While Freud was studying in Paris his interest in hypnosis increased, and when he was back in Vienna after a brief stay in Berlin he gave the Society of Medicine an account of what he had seen and learned in Paris. In *An Autobiographical Study* he describes the reactions of an old Viennese surgeon to his description of case studies of male hysteria: 'But, my dear sir, how can you talk such nonsense? *Hysteron* [*sic*] means the uterus. So how can a man be hysterical?' (ibid., p. 15).

At Meynert's suggestion he tried to find in Vienna cases similar to those he had described, and to present them to the Society of Medicine, but once again the Society's scepticism thwarted him: they were not even interested in a case of male hysteria in a patient suffering from myasthenia. Many years later Freud attributed their indifference to the fact that his research took a direction that was not acceptable to con-temporary physicians who had been taught to observe ana-tomical, physical and chemical factors only. In their view psychic factors were not worthy of scientific investigation. They dismissed the symptoms of hysterical neurosis as simulations and hypnosis as an imposture. Even psychiatrists who were accustomed to very unusual, often dramatic, psychic manifestations were extremely unwilling to discuss these matters in detail, or allow that there might be a connection between their work and that of Freud. They were content merely to try to ascribe a variety of pathological symptoms to somatic, anatomic, or chemical causes. In a materialistic, or rather mechanistic, age medicine had cer-tainly made formidable progress, but it was also shortsighted in failing to appreciate what was in Freud's view the most important and difficult problem of human existence.

Because of his theories on male hysteria and the way in which paralysis could be induced by suggestion Freud was again forced to join the ranks of the opposition — a situation which, as we have seen, he found stimulating. Moreover, his moral integrity and professional scrupulousness led him to side with 'suffering humanity' to a greater extent than he was willing to admit: 'Anyone who wanted to make a living from the treatment of nerve-patients must clearly be able to do something to help them . . . My therapeutic arsenal contained only two weapons, electrotherapy and hypnosis, for pre-scribing a visit to a hydropathic establishment after a single consultation was an inadequate source of income' (*An Auto-biographical Study*, standard edn, vol. XX, p. 16).

It was not so much a question of income which induced Freud to abandon traditional therapeutic methods as his awareness of their inefficacy and of the unscientific nature of the prescriptions then in use:

> My knowledge of electrotherapy was derived from W. Erb's text-book, which provided detailed instructions for the treat-ment of all the symptoms of nervous diseases. Unluckily I was soon driven to see that following these instructions was of no help whatever and that what I had taken for an epitome of exact observations was merely the construction of phantasy. The realization that the work of the greatest name in German neuropathology had no more relation to reality than some 'Egyptian' dream-book, such as are sold in cheap bookshops, was painful, but it helped to rid me of yet another piece of innocent faith in authority by which I was still obsessed. So I put my electrical apparatus aside, even before Möbius had solved the problem by explaining that the successes of electric treatment in nervous disorders (in so far as there were any) were the effect of suggestion on the part of the physician. (Ibid.)

Freud and Bernheim

Again it was Freud's intellectual integrity and his interest in research which made him go to Nancy to perfect his hypnosis technique after three years as a practising physician (1886—9). As we have seen, there were other well-known doctors whose views differed from those of disciples of the Charcot school but who were evincing a new scientific interest in hypnosis at the time. Freud got in touch with Liébeault and Bernheim and was impressed by two basic aspects of the Nancy school: the ageing Liébeault's concern for human suffering which led

him to spend a great deal of time with his patients, listening to
their experiences and memories, and Bernheim's experiments
which confirmed some of Freud's own doubts concerning
Charcot's theories and methods.

Freud agreed with Bernheim and disagreed with Charcot
on the following points:

> Contrary to Charcot's view, it is a mistake to believe that
> hypnosis can only be used on hysterics because they are
> generally considered to be not entirely normal, that is,
> they are thought to have a hereditary or acquired mental
> weakness. Hypnosis can be applied with equal success to
> non-hysterics.
>
> It is not necessary, as Charcot maintained, to induce a
> profound hypnotic trance in the patient so as to make
> him behave in a certain way or recall certain past events,
> etc. This can be achieved under light hypnosis or even by
> talking to the patient while he is awake. The hypnotic
> state is no more than a light slumber induced by the
> hypnotist.
>
> Not all patients, hysterical or otherwise, can be hypnotized.

Freud disagreed with Bernheim on one crucial point, as is
evident from his preface to Bernheim's work which he
translated and first presented to the German-speaking public
in 1889. The basic theory of the Nancy school was that
everything which occurred under hypnosis was caused by the
physician's power of suggestion over the patient. Although
Freud was convinced that certain pathological symptoms are
caused by psychic and not organic phenomena and will thus
respond to psychic therapy, he was unwilling to admit that it
was a matter of suggestion, or rather that it was nothing but
suggestion, for this would leave unsolved the question of
what exactly this suggestion was and of how it affected the
psyche.

In his preface to the 1896 edition Freud clearly restated his viewpoint. Bernheim, he observed, ascribes all phenomena to suggestion but never explains how suggestion itself operates, as though there were no need to explain it. Freud maintained — and on this point he was closer to Charcot — that hysterical symptoms, even when they are induced by hypnotic suggestion, are of a specific nature which is not derived from suggestion, and that it is this nature that should be investigated in order to understand the cause and significance of symptoms.

Freud and Breuer

Between 1889 and 1895 Freud treated his patients by hypnosis with occasional use of other contemporary methods, in which, however, he had little faith, such as hydrotherapy, massage and electrotherapy. Although he was still using Bernheim's method of light hypnosis and hypnotic suggestion to induce the patient to abandon the symptoms which afflicted him, he was beginning to lose faith in hypnotic therapy for a variety of reasons.

From the outset Freud's scientific yet human approach led him to use hypnosis in a different way; he was not content just to put the patient to sleep and to suggest that he abandon his symptoms:

> I used it for questioning the patient upon the origin of his symptom, which in his waking state he could often describe only very imperfectly or not at all. Not only did this method seem more effective than bald suggestive commands or prohibitions, but it also satisfied the curiosity of the physician, who, after all, had a right to learn something of the origin of the phenomenon which he strove to remove by the monotonous procedure of suggestion. (*An Autobiographical Study*, standard edn, vol. XX, p. 19)

This stress on the *monotony* of the suggestive method is typical of Freud. He was never content with therapeutic results but always wanted to get to the root cause.

At this time Freud was in close contact with Breuer, a famous Viennese surgeon and an old friend of the Freud family. It was through Breuer, or rather as a result of Freud's elaboration of one of Breuer's experiments, that Freud made the transition from hypnotic suggestion to the 'cathartic method' and from this to psychoanalysis.

Freud had met Breuer at Brücke's physiology laboratory while he was a student, that is, eight years before launching into private practice. Breuer was 15 years older than Freud and already one of the most highly regarded family doctors in Vienna and an established scientist and researcher. The two men became friends and developed a profound respect for one another, which consisted in admiration and deference on Freud's part and affectionate patronage and friendly encouragement on Breuer's. The latter was generous with his advice and with financial backing, and for many years their scientific interests were identical.

Even before Freud's expedition to Paris, in November 1882 to be precise, Breuer had told him about the case of a young hysteric, Bertha Pappenheim (later known as Anna O.), whom he had treated between 1880 and 1882. The case made a great impression on Freud and while he was in Paris he mentioned it to Charcot. The 'Master', however, was not particularly interested. One senses a note of irony in Freud's manner of addressing the Grand Magician of Hysteria thus, because of his refusal to investigate a case which proved crucial for a better understanding of hysteria and its symptoms. Freud was not deterred by this indifference:

When I was back in Vienna I turned once more to Breuer's observation and made him tell me more about it. The patient had been a young girl of unusual education and gifts, who had fallen ill while she was nursing her father, of whom she was devotedly fond. When Breuer took over her case it presented a variegated picture of paralyses and contractures, inhibitions and states of mental confusion. A chance observation showed her physician that she could be relieved of these clouded states of consciousness if she was induced to express in words the affective phantasy by which she was at the moment dominated. (Ibid., p. 20)

The 'chance observation' was the following: according to Breuer's account in *Studies on Hysteria,* the patient had two quite distinct states of consciousness which alternated very frequently and without warning and became more and more differentiated in the course of the illness. In the first she recognized her surroundings, was sad and anxious but relatively normal, and in the second she hallucinated and 'misbehaved', throwing cushions at people, swearing, tearing buttons off her underclothes, etc. She thought she saw terrifying black snakes in her ribbons or in anything looking remotely like them. Because she always reacted out loud to whatever she saw in her hallucinations, sometimes sounding like a tragic actress, the people round about her knew more or less what form they took. These attacks were followed by periods of drowsiness and towards evening she would fall into a deep sleep, a sort of auto-hypnosis, which she called her clouds. After an hour or so she would wake up and when asked to explain what had upset her, at the mention of an image or a word she had used during a crisis she would begin to talk about some incident from her past, at first in a confused fashion but gradually becoming more explicit. Breuer first visited her during the evening period of auto-hypnosis and later induced this state artificially to accelerate her recovery. The effect of his interventions, which the patient called the 'talking cure' or 'chimney sweeping', became more and more obvious.

From this discovery, Breuer arrived at a new method of treatment. He put her into deep hypnosis and made her tell him each time what it was that was oppressing her mind. After the attacks of depressive confusion had been overcome in this way, he employed the same procedure for removing her inhibitions and physical disorders. In her waking state the girl could no more describe than other patients how her symptoms had arisen, and she could discover no link between them and any experiences of her life. In hypnosis she immediately revealed the missing connection. It turned out that all of her symptoms went back to moving events which she had experienced while nursing her father; that is to say, her symptoms had a meaning and were residues or reminiscences of those emotional situations. It turned out in most instances that there had been some thought or impulse which she had to suppress while she was by her father's sick-bed, and that, in place of it, as a substitute for it, the symptom had afterwards appeared. But as a rule the symptom was not the precipitate of a single such 'traumatic' scene, but the result of a summation of a number of similar situations. When the patient recalled a situation of this kind in a hallucinatory way under hypnosis and carried through to its conclusion, with a free expression of emotion, the mental act which she had originally suppressed, the symptom was wiped away and did not return. By this procedure Breuer succeeded, after long and painful efforts, in relieving his patient of all her symptoms. (Ibid.)

The significant theoretical assumptions which Freud and Breuer derived from this case were published in *On the Psychical Mechanism of Hysterical Phenomena: Preliminary Communication* (1893). They can be summed up as follows:

Symptoms which appear in hysteria and can be artificially induced by hypnosis should not be seen as being suggested by the doctor. Indeed, in the case of Anna O., Breuer was confronted with a patient suffering from

spontaneous autohypnosis and in this state she referred
to facts of which he knew nothing but which her family
later confirmed.

Such symptoms are *equivalents* for emotions caused by
psychic traumas experienced by the patient, emotions
that did not find a satisfactory outlet and therefore
remained in the psyche like some foreign body, hinder-
ing the normal activity of the psyche.

When the patient is awake he does not remember the cause
of the trauma, or does so only with difficulty, or if the
doctor applies verbal pressure.

The difference between Freud and Breuer

Freud and Breuer differed mainly in their interpretation of
the significance of the patient's 'inability to remember'. In the
Preliminary Communication the two interpretations appear
side by side. Breuer believed that the 'inability to remember'
which would in due course find a permanent outlet in the
patient's symptoms could be explained by the fact that the
initial trauma had occurred in a 'hypnoid state'. In other
words, according to him, such patients have a tendency to
split their personality and lead two different existences, as it
were. This is precisely what happened to Anna O.

There were two psychical characteristics present in the girl
while she was still completely healthy which acted as pre-
disposing causes for her subsequent hysterical illness:

1 Her monotonous family life and the absence of adequate
   intellectual occupation left her with an unemployed sur-
   plus of mental liveliness and energy, and this found an
   outlet in the constant activity of her imagination.
2 This led to a habit of day-dreaming (her 'private theatre')

which laid the foundations for the dissociation of her
mental personality.

(*Studies on Hysteria*, standard edn, vol. II, p. 41)

Freud did not deny that a predisposition for hysteria
existed, but he asserted that according to his own clinical
experience this 'inability to remember' had nothing to do
with a psychic predisposition to eliminate certain significant
subjects from consciousness, but was caused by the inhibition
of the patient who did not wish to have a conscious memory
of a painful experience: 'We have found, however, that a
severe trauma (such as occurs in a traumatic neurosis) or a
laborious suppression (as of a sexual affect, for instance) can
bring about a splitting-off of groups of ideas even in people
who are in other respects unaffected; and this would be the
mechanism of *psychically acquired* hysteria' (ibid., p. 12). To
this group belong the cases of patients who

> have not reacted to a psychical trauma because the nature of
> the trauma excluded a reaction, as in the case of the apparently
> irreparable loss of a loved person or because social circum-
> stances made a reaction impossible or because it was a
> question of things which the patient wished to forget, and
> therefore intentionally repressed from his conscious thought
> and inhibited and suppressed. It is precisely distressing things
> of this kind that, under hypnosis, we find are the basis of
> hysterical phenomena (e.g. hysterical deliria in saints and
> nuns, continent women and well-brought-up children). (Ibid.,
> pp. 10–11)

This is the first time the term *repression* appears in the
analytic sense of the word and we feel that Freud's use of it
should be stressed because it constitutes the basic distinction
between Freud and Breuer and between Freud and the
'French school', as Freud himself was later to explain in 'The
Psycho-Analytic View of Psychogenic Disturbance of Vision'

(1910). In this essay on the phenomenon of hysterical blindness Freud asks: 'How does it happen that such people develop the unconscious "autosuggestion" that they are blind, while nevertheless they see in their unconscious?' (standard edn, vol. XI, p. 212). The French school's answer to this question is that people with a hysterical predisposition are prone to dissociation — to a dissolution of links with psychic experience — so that many unconscious processes never reach their consciousness. Freud, on the other hand, asserts that

> Psychoanalysis, too, accepts the assumptions of dissociation and the unconscious, but relates them differently to each other. Its view is a dynamic one, which traces mental life back to an interplay between forces that favour or inhibit one another. If in any instance one group of ideas remains in the unconscious, psychoanalysis does not infer that there is a constitutional incapacity for synthesis which is showing itself in this particular dissociation, but maintains that the isolation and state of unconsciousness of this group of ideas have been caused by an active opposition on the part of other groups. The process owing to which it has met with this fate is known as 'repression' and we regard it as something analogous to a condemnatory judgement in the field of logic. Psychoanalysis points out that repressions of this kind play an extraordinarily important part in our mental life, but that they may also frequently fail and that such failures of repression are the precondition of the formation of symptoms. (Ibid., p. 213)

This passage summarizes the experimental and theoretical climate which either preceded or was even contemporary with Freud's research. We have repeatedly seen that the idea of an unconscious, of alternative or multiple personalities mysteriously inhabiting the same individual and of the impact of psychic phenomena on organic symptoms, formed part of the culture of the time. Freud's originality consists in having located these phenomena in a dynamic and significant context and shown them to be valid psychic mechanisms even in normal human beings. When Charcot and Breuer postulated a deficiency in the integrating processes of the ego (Breuer's *hypnoid state,* Charcot's *misère psychologique*) they placed the patient suffering from mental disturbance (the 'nervous person' as the neurotic was then called) in a separate category, isolating him from normal people. According to Freud, on the contrary, the mechanism by which the painful affect is resisted (the concept of repression is clearly apparent here) and relegated to a separate (unconscious) zone, where it continues none the less to exert its disturbing influence, is part of the normal psyche. Indeed we all tend to forget more easily the things we would rather not remember. Thus the difference between 'nervous' and normal people consists in the degree to which this repression is successful. The hysterical symptom refers directly or indirectly or even symbolically to the painful topic that has been previously repressed and is seeking expression.

The method discovered by Breuer and perfected by Freud came to be known as the 'cathartic' or purifying method: 'Breuer spoke of our method as *cathartic*; its therapeutic aim was explained as being to provide that the accumulated affect used for maintaining the symptom, which had got onto the wrong lines, as it were, become stuck there, should be directed onto the normal path along which it could obtain discharge (or *abreaction*)' (*An Autobiographical Study,* standard edn, vol. XX, p. 22).

Chronology

1885—6   From October 1885 until February 1886 Freud is in Paris and attends Charcot's courses at the Salpêtrière studying hysterical symptoms and their treatment by hypnosis and suggestion. On 25 April he sets up a private practice in Vienna. In September he marries Martha Bernays. He publishes his translation of Charcot's *Leçons sur les maladies du système nerveux.*

1887   He begins to use hypnosis in his private practice.

1888   He publishes his translation of Bernheim's *De la suggestion et de ses applications à la thérapeutique,* and specifies in the introduction the points on which he and Breuer disagree.

1889   Visits Bernheim and Liébeault at Nancy.

1893   In collaboration with Breuer he publishes *On the Psychical Mechanism of Hysterical Phenomena: Preliminary Communication* (*Studies on Hysteria,* part I).

5

From the Cathartic Method to Psychoanalysis

Freud's first clinical cases

The clinical case studies which Freud and Breuer carried out independently between 1886 and 1895 were published collectively under their joint signatures in *Studies on Hysteria,* a work of the utmost interest not only because it marks the common starting-point of both authors (the therapeutic advantages of the *talking cure* over the *monotony* of hypnotic suggestion) but also because it shows how Freud gradually progressed towards true psychoanalysis.

Freud described these as 'groping' years, when the romantic image of an instant genius unhesitatingly striding towards his goal could not have been further from the truth. For Freud moved between clinical observations and theoretical speculations which sometimes confirmed one another and sometimes did not, and the definitive solution lay always in the future.

From the *Preliminary Communication* written by Freud and Breuer jointly in 1892 to 'The Psychotherapy of Hysteria', the final essay in the volume, written by Freud in 1895, one can trace Freud's gradual separation from Breuer and the evolution of his own particular method of treating his patients. These clinical cases read like short stories, a fact that caused Freud some embarrassment and compelled him to justify himself:

> I have not always been a psychotherapist. Like other neuro-pathologists, I was trained to employ local diagnoses and electro-prognosis, and it still strikes me myself as strange that the case histories I write should read like short stories and that, as one might say, they lack the serious stamp of science. I must console myself with the reflection that the nature of the subject is evidently responsible for this, rather than any preference of my own. The fact is that local diagnosis and electrical reactions lead nowhere in the study of hysteria, whereas a detailed description of mental processes such as we are accustomed to find in the works of imaginative writers enables me, with the use of a few psychological formulas, to obtain at least some kind of insight into the course of that affection. Case histories of this kind are intended to be judged like psychiatric ones; they have, however, one advantage over the latter, namely an intimate connection between the story of the patient's sufferings and the symptoms of his illness — a connection for which we still search in vain in the biographies of other psychoses. (*Studies on Hysteria*, standard edn, vol. II, pp. 160—1)

Freud's use of *analysis* differs from hypnotic suggestion in that he aimed to understand and make explicit, and not just force the patient to abandon his symptoms. This was the most important aspect of his method. We will now consider certain aspects of several case histories in dealing with which Freud came to formulate his psychoanalytical method.

Frau Emmy von N.

In *Studies on Hysteria* Emmy von N. is described as a young-looking lady in her forties of above-average intellect and culture who consulted Freud about some rather disturbing symptoms she had: cramp, depression, phobias, tics and fits of hysterical delirium, that is, recurrent hallucinations of a horrifying kind from which she tried to protect herself by shrieking 'Keep still! — Don't say anything! — Don't touch me', and so on. Afterwards she would resume her normal behaviour as though unaware of what had happened. Freud began his treatment of the patient with the 'mixed method': warm baths, massage, hypnotic suggestion and the cathartic method, whereby he tried to retrace the traumatic event which had caused the disorder by examining what she said when under hypnosis. Freud learned many important facts from this case:

1   Given the patient's intelligence and culture, her common sense and initiative, he felt she confirmed his theory that hysteria is not restricted to congenitally 'degenerate' minds.

2   His theory that symptoms are the expression of emotions which have not found an outlet at the time of the trauma was vindicated. In this case it was not always easy to interpret these expressions. For instance, the patient would stretch her hands out in front of her, with her fingers wide apart and contorted in a gesture of evident terror, as if to fend off something she had previously experienced. The process was often more complicated: memories of the original trauma usually only expressed themselves as the merest hint in a symptom, or even as their exact opposite. For instance, during the convalescence of a sick daughter the patient forced herself to be completely silent so as not to disturb the invalid, but this led to the fear that she might nevertheless make a noise that would waken the child. In her ensuing mental confusion the latter idea, instead of being repressed, took precedence, and to her horror she found herself uttering a series of little cries against her will, like those she resorted to when she felt frightened or mentally threatened.

3   He realized that orders given to the patient when under hypnosis — for example, telling her to stop being afraid of insects or toads, or giving her instructions as to how to behave — did not have the desired effect: the patient seemed to cling obstinately to her morbid symptoms and to set up a resistance to the suggestive process:

> I invariably observed a strained and dissatisfied expression on her face; and when, at the end of the hypnosis, I asked her whether she would still be afraid of the animal, she would answer: 'No — since you insist.' A promise like this, based only on her obedience to me, never met with any success, any more than did the many general injunctions which I laid upon her, instead of which I might just as well have repeated the single suggestion that she should get well. (Ibid., p. 99)

Despite the patient's exceptionally sincere and open disposition in everyday life and despite her wish to be frank and docile in her dealings with her doctor, she set up an obvious resistance to 'recovery' as well as a resistance to 'remembering': indeed, even under hypnosis, as her memory drew closer to a painful subject she would tend to provide 'incomplete evidence'. Thus it would seem that the phenomenon of resistance operates even under hypnosis.

4   According to Freud the cure was an apparent success, but not a lasting one. In his account of this case he ascribes his failure to the patient's unconscious resistance, as a result of which information which was obtained from her directly or under hypnosis about her past history never touched on the vital and probably the most important matter, the sexual element, which she totally omitted from all her confessions: 'I cannot help suspecting that this woman who was so passionate and so capable of strong feelings had not won her victory over her sexual needs without severe struggles, and that at times her attempts at suppressing this most powerful

of all instincts had exposed her to severe mental exhaustion' (ibid., p. 103). On the other hand, the symptoms whose psychic evolution Freud was able to trace from their beginning tended to disappear: 'I must add that only those symptoms of which I carried out a psychical analysis were really permanently removed' (ibid., p. 101).

5   He realized the importance of letting the patient's memories and fantasies flow freely even when these did not appear to have anything to do with the symptom or with each other. He found that by allowing the free association of ideas, vivid memories would emerge and give meaning to what had preceded them.

Miss Lucy R.

The main features of the second case are as follows: Miss Lucy, a governess in her thirties, consulted Freud for chronic rhinitis, depression, fatigue, loss of appetite and sense of weariness, and olfactory hallucinations — she was almost continually obsessed by the smell of burnt pudding. The treatment was not as regular as it might have been and her visits had to be fitted in between one patient and another. Miss Lucy did not fall into a state of trance when Freud tried to hypnotize her. Therefore he had to abandon hypnosis and the use of the 'extended memory' which it induces. Here is Freud's own account of his important change of method. Since Miss Lucy, like certain other patients was not amenable to hypnotism:

> I was accordingly faced with the choice of either abandoning the cathartic method . . . or of venturing on the experiment of employing the method without somnambulism . . . Moreover, I soon dropped the practice of making tests to show the degree of hypnosis reached, since in quite a number of cases this roused the patients' resistance and shook their confidence

in me, which I needed for carrying out the more important
psychical work. Furthermore, I soon began to tire of issuing
assurances and commands such as: 'You are going to sleep!
. . . sleep!' and of hearing the patient, as so often happened
when the degree of hypnosis was light, remonstrate with me:
'But, doctor, I'm not asleep', and of having to make highly
ticklish distinctions: 'I don't mean ordinary sleep; I mean
hypnosis. As you see, you are hypnotized, you can't open
your eyes', etc. 'and in any case there's no need for you to go
to sleep', and so on. I feel sure that many other physicians
who practise psychotherapy can get out of such difficulties
with more skill than I can. If so, they may adopt some
procedure other than mine. It seems to me, however, that if
one can reckon with such frequency on finding oneself in an
embarrassing situation through the use of a particular word,
one will be wise to avoid both the word and the embarrassment. When therefore, my first attempt did not lead either to
somnabulism or to a degree of hypnosis involving marked
physical changes, I ostensibly dropped hypnosis, and only
asked for 'concentration', and I ordered the patient to lie
down and deliberately shut his eyes as a means of achieving
this 'concentration'. (Ibid., pp. 108—9)

If, once the patient was 'concentrating', he had some difficulty in evoking memories of a pathogenic nature, Freud
would resort to a method he had learned from Bernheim at
Nancy, which consisted in exerting a gentle pressure with his
fingers on the patient's forehead, urging him to remember, or
rather to *let his thoughts flow freely and to describe everything that came into his head, whether fantasies, memories, or
sensations.*

After 1903 Freud stopped using this method because it
proved to have disastrous consequences. Indeed, he later
explicitly recommended that all physical contact with the
patient should be avoided during analysis ('On Beginning the
Treatment (Further Recommendations on the Technique of

Psycho-Analysis)'). However, when he employed this method he had probably not yet had any evidence of the erotic element which enters into the relationship between doctor and patient, nor was he aware of such a possibility and still less of the way in which it might be overcome or even be used as an important tool in psychoanalysis.

On the other hand, he never abandoned the so-called 'basic rule' of asking the patient to report as freely as possible everything going through his head, without in any way censuring his images, fantasies, or thoughts. This fundamentally important aspect of Freud's technique is what most distinguishes it from hypnosis. It is worth quoting Freud's own words on the technique of *free association* which he developed during his early clinical cases, and established as a theory. He wrote in 1913:

> What subject-matter the treatment begins with is on the whole immaterial, whether with the patient's life-story, with a history of the illness or with recollections of childhood; but in any case the patient must be left to talk, and the choice of subject left to him. One says to him, therefore, 'Before I can say anything to you, I must know a great deal about you; please tell me what you know about yourself'.
>
> The only exception to this concerns the fundamental rule of psycho-analytic technique which the patient must observe. This must be imparted to him at the very beginning: 'One thing more, before you begin. Your talk with me must differ in one respect from ordinary conversation. Whereas usually you rightly try to keep the threads of your story together and to exclude all intruding associations and side-issues so as not to wander too far from the point, here you must proceed differently. You will notice that as you relate things various ideas will occur to you which you feel inclined to put aside with certain criticisms and objections. You will be tempted to say to yourself: 'This or that has no connection here, or it is quite unimportant, or it is nonsensical, so it cannot be

necessary to mention it.' Never give in to these objections, but mention it even if you feel a disinclination against it, or indeed, just because of this . . . So say whatever goes through your mind. ('On beginning the treatment', standard edn, vol. XII, pp. 134—5)

What emerges clearly from these early cases is that despite the therapist's encouragement and the patient's willingness to comply, there exists a 'counter-will' in the patient which makes him break away from the basis rule, and it is precisely the reason for this which has to be investigated:

This business of enlarging what was supposed to be a restricted consciousness was laborious — far more so, at least, than an investigation during somnambulism. But it nevertheless made me independent of somnambulism, and gave me insight into the motives which often determine the 'forgetting' of memories. I can affirm that this forgetting is often intentional and desired; and its success is never more than *apparent*. (*Studies on Hysteria*, standard edn, vol. II, p. 111)

In the final chapter of *Studies on Hysteria* the connection between the patient's resistance and the psychic force which generates the symptom is even more explicitly expressed:

Experiences like this made me think that it would in fact be possible for the pathogenic groups of ideas, that were after all certainly present, to be brought to light by mere insistence; and since this insistence involved effort on my part and so suggested the idea that I had to overcome a resistance, the situation led me at once to the theory that *by means of my psychical work I had to overcome a psychical force in the patients which was opposed to the pathogenic ideas becoming conscious (being remembered)*. A new understanding seemed to open before my eyes when it occurred to me that this must no doubt be the same psychical force that had played a part in

the generating of the hysterical symptom and had at that time
prevented the pathogenic idea from becoming conscious.
(Ibid., p. 268)

Katharina

The case of Katharina (ibid., pp. 125—34), an 18-year-old
chambermaid in a boarding house whom Freud met by
chance during a holiday in the mountains, cannot of course
be seen as a *psychoanalytic cure*. Freud reports the case with
the relish of a researcher who finds a chance corroboration of
a theory, but at the same time admits the inconclusive nature
of his findings. Katharina suffered from anxiety and recurrent
hallucinations which she described to Freud in the course of a
lengthy conversation. He was able to relate these symptoms
to a traumatic incident in her distant past: her father had tried
to rape her. It is interesting to note that in his original account
Freud refers to an uncle rather than to the father, and it was
not until 1924, in a footnote added to the case history, that he
lifted 'the veil of discretion' to reveal the truth. He also refers
to Katharina's inability to cope with sexual experiences at the
early age at which this first traumatic episode occurred, and
uses terms such as 'innocence' and the 'pre-sexual stage'. The
notion of infantile sexuality was still foreign to Freud, while
his personal resistance to the idea of an Oedipus complex was
responsible for his reticence. However, the most significant
factor of the case is Freud's comment that it was 'not so much
an analysed case of hysteria as a case solved by guessing'. The
consequences were frustrating: 'The patient agreed that what
I interpolated into her story was probably true, but she was
not in a position to recognize it as something she had
experienced' (ibid., p. 133). The inconclusive outcome was
the result of the casual way in which the case was presented to
him, as well as of his own purely intellectual concern with it.
This confirms Freud's view that it is not so much the process

of *understanding* which resolves the patient's problems as the chance to re-enact emotively the traumas of the past in his relationship with the physician, and thus re-establish the link between the ego and the material which was repressed from consciousness.

Later, in the essay '"Wild" Psycho-Analysis', Freud was most explicit on the subject of this form of treatment and its limitations:

> It is a long superseded idea, and one derived from superficial appearances, that the patient suffers from a sort of ignorance, and that if one removes this ignorance by giving him information (about the causal connection of his illness with his life, about his experiences in childhood, and so on) he is bound to recover. The pathological factor is not his ignorance in itself but the root of this ignorance in his *inner resistances*; it was they that first called this ignorance into being, and they still maintain it now. (Standard edn, vol. XI, p. 225)

Fraulein Elisabeth von R.

A 24-year-old girl consulted Freud for violent pains in her legs which were not of an organic nature but which made her unable to walk. She seemed intelligent and ambitious but had recently experienced a great deal of suffering: her dearly loved father had died, her mother had been seriously ill, her favourite sister had died of a miscarriage and she had been separated from another sister by the latter's marriage.

In *Studies on Hysteria* Freud describes how Elizabeth, like Miss Lucy, resisted hypnosis so he resorted to the *concentration* method with increased confidence. He had now become convinced that a patient's failure to remember corresponded to a reluctance to remember or to his resistance, and that this resistance could throw light on the repressed material.

As in the case of Miss Lucy he noticed when he examined a symptom that what he discovered was not an isolated traumatic experience but a series of similar experiences — in other words, the symptom is *overdetermined*. Furthermore, it became clear that the appearance or reappearance of a symptom is not caused by a new trauma but by the *memory* of an earlier trauma. For instance, Elizabeth's resistance and hesitation when she was about to touch on a subject which she found painful and dangerous to recall was so great that the pains in her legs increased at these times. It was as though she relived the disagreeable experience during the session in a way that was akin to remembering.

By the time he came to write the last chapter of the *Studies*, entitled 'The Psychotherapy of Hysteria', Freud seems to have become technically and metapsychologically assured. The importance of his basic rule of not interrupting the patient's free association of ideas had been confirmed, and the various reactions of the patient, such as resistance, had been explained. The analyst no longer had the role of the pedagogue or influenced the patient by means of suggestion and the analytical process had been defined in terms of a struggle against resistance, in which a therapeutic investigation is carried out with the patient's collaboration.

First intuitions about the importance of transference

In this last chapter Freud gives a detailed account of a particular form of resistance which he had overlooked and been unwilling to recognize while absorbed in his research into the circumstances which unconsciously cause symptoms. While stressing the importance of the relationship between the patient and the analyst, Freud admits that if it becomes an uneasy one it must 'unfortunately' be dealt with, because otherwise it can impede the patient's free association and produce resistance. Thus, however 'tiresome' it might be, the patient must be made aware of the situation and this new development included in the work of interpretation (*Studies on Hysteria*, standard edn, vol. II, pp. 301–4). From this first observation Freud realized that by demonstrating a resistance to the therapist the patient *re-enacts* within this relationship certain conflictual situations which have been significant in his own life. It is therefore necessary to analyse the relationship between the patient and the analyst in order to establish the nature of it, and the way in which the patient is *transferring* on to the analyst. Freud calls *false connections* those feelings which a patient has experienced in the past for a given person and later transfers to the analyst so that they become falsely connected to the person of the analyst. These feelings may be of various kinds: they may be hostile and translated into resistance to treatment, or erotic, troubling and so embarrassing to the patient as to make him want to curtail treatment, or they can be expressed as a direct 're-enactment' during the sessions.

By the time he had finished writing *Studies on Hysteria* Freud was already aware of the crucial importance of what takes place during therapeutic sessions, not only because any disruption in the patient—analyst relationship has an impact on the process itself, but also because the analysis of what takes place brings to light forgotten associations and thus reactivates the pathogenic process. In 1901 Freud gave an account of the case history of Dora, a young girl who consulted Freud for hysterical symptoms of various kinds, who suddenly interrupted treatment after barely three months of otherwise highly satisfactory therapy. Freud discusses the problem of *transference* and of *acting out* during the treatment, which takes the place of remembering:

Transference is the one thing the presence of which has to be detected almost without assistance and with only the slightest clues to go upon, while at the same time the risk of making arbitrary inferences has to be avoided. Nevertheless, transference cannot be evaded, since use is made of it in setting up all the obstacles that make the material inaccessible to treatment, and since it is only after the transference has been resolved that a patient arrives at a sense of conviction of the validity of the connections which have been constructed during the analysis ... Transference, which seems ordained to be the greatest obstacle to psycho-analysis, becomes its most powerful ally, if its presence can be detected each time and explained to the patient. ('Fragment of an analysis of a case of hysteria', standard edn, vol. VII, pp. 116–17)

Commenting on the abrupt termination of the treatment, Freud admits that if he had paid more attention to the transference — or to the kind of fantasies the patient transferred on to him — he might have made the patient aware of it and thus prevented her abandoning him as she had previously abandoned the object of her erotic fantasies:

> In this way the transference took me unawares, and, because of the unknown quantity in me which reminded Dora of Herr K., she took her revenge on me as she wanted to take her revenge on him, and deserted me as she believed herself to have been deceived and deserted by him. Thus she *acted out* an essential part of her recollections and phantasies instead of reproducing it in the treatment. (Ibid., p. 119)

Later, in 'The Dynamics of Transference' (1912), Freud was to stress the decisive role transference plays in analysis. In this essay he points out how essential it is to analyse not only the positive transference whereby tender and affectionate feelings are transferred on to the analyst, but also the negative transference of aggressive, hostile feelings, and he notes that the patient can experience these ambivalent emotions simultaneously and that it is the analyst's task to make the patient aware of them.

These feelings are no more than a re-enactment, a repetition of certain ways the patient has of relating, and they are derived from a much earlier stage of the patient's life than that in which the actual patient—analyst relationship occurs. Thus as they occur they can reveal the particular way in which an individual reacted to his first infantile love-object. Obviously the process is not without its difficulties, but it is precisely through the study of the difficulties — or resistances — involved in transference that the characteristics of a particular patient's reactions emerge, reactions which are partly conscious and accessible to him and partly unconscious. In other words, during his development some of his reactions have been withheld, removed from his conscious mind, and can only express themselves in the form of fantasies, or they may have become completely buried in the unconscious.

Later still, in 'Remembering, Repeating and Working-Through' (1914), Freud explained in great detail the radical transformation in the analytical method which was the result of a dialectic confrontation of his theoretical hypotheses with clinical observation. From now on the main purpose of analysis would no longer be to enable the patient to recall the traumatic *event* which had given rise to the repression and the symptoms, but to analyse the resistances acted out during therapy. This is how Freud himself sums up the process:

It seems to me not unnecessary to keep on reminding students of the far-reaching changes which psycho-analytic technique has undergone since its first beginnings. In its first phase — that of Breuer's catharsis — it consisted in bringing directly into focus the moment at which the symptom was formed and in persistently endeavouring to reproduce the mental processes involved in that situation, in order to direct their discharge along the path of conscious activity. Remembering and abreacting, with the help of the hypnotic state, were what was at that time aimed at. Next, when hypnosis had been given up, the task became one of discovering from the patient's free associations what he failed to remember. The resistance was to be circumvented by the work of interpretation and by making its results known to the patient. The situations which had given rise to the formation of the symptom and the other situations which lay behind the moment at which the illness broke out retained their place as the focus of interest; but the element of abreaction receded into the background and seemed to be replaced by the expenditure of work which the patient had to make in being obliged to overcome his criticism of his free associations, in accordance with the fundamental rule of psycho-analysis. Finally, there was evolved the consistent technique used today, in which the analyst gives up the attempt to bring a particular moment or problem into focus. He contents himself with studying whatever is present for the time being on the surface of the patient's mind, and he employs the art of interpretation mainly for the purpose of recognizing the resistances which appear there, and making them conscious to the patient. (Standard edn, vol. XII, p. 147)

Further on he specifies that the patient may well remember nothing at all of what he had forgotten and repressed or he may feel the need to *act out* elements of this forgotten or repressed material during the session:

For instance, the patient does not say that he remembers that he used to be defiant and critical towards his parents' authority; instead, he behaves in that way to the doctor. He does not remember how he came to a helpless and hopeless deadlock in his infantile sexual researches; but he produces a mass of confused dreams and associations, complains that he cannot succeed in anything and asserts that he is fated never to carry through what he undertakes. He does not remember having been intensely ashamed of certain sexual activities and afraid of their being found out; but he makes it clear that he is ashamed of the treatment on which he is now embarked and tries to keep it secret from everybody. And so on. (Ibid., p. 150)

Chronology

1892—5   During these years Freud established the basic principles of his method and published them in an essay entitled 'The Psychotherapy of Hysteria', which constitutes the final chapter of *Studies on Hysteria* which he wrote in collaboration with Breuer.

6

From Error to Explanation

Freud's mistake

By the end of *Studies on Hysteria* the psychoanalytic method may be said to have taken on a definite character which distinguishes it both from the now-abandoned hypnotic method and from the cathartic method. Freud was now convinced that the cases he had examined proved that hysterical phenomena and obsessional neuroses were all caused by *sexual trauma*, more specifically by the sexual seduction of the patient in early childhood by an adult. Indeed, information gleaned from patients' free association under analysis, as they delved deeper and deeper into their 'memories', seemed to confirm this hypothesis and establish it as a certainty. Freud himself described how his conviction grew in a letter to Fliess dated 30 May 1893 in which he considers it 'quite a possibility' that forgotten and repressed sexual traumas were the prime source of disturbances: 'I see quite a possibility of filling another gap in the sexual aetiology of the neuroses ... I have analysed two such cases, and the cause was an apprehensive terror of sexuality, against a background of things they had seen or heard and only half-understood; thus the aetiology was purely emotional, but still of a sexual nature' (*The Origins of Psycho-Analysis*, p. 73). In another letter written to Fliess two years later on 2 November 1895 this hypothesis is announced as a certainty:

> Dear Wilhelm,
> . . . Have I revealed the great clinical secret to you, either in writing or by word of mouth? Hysteria is the consequence of a pre-sexual *sexual shock*. Obsessional neurosis is the consequence of pre-sexual *sexual pleasure* later transformed into guilt. (Ibid., p. 120)

We note that Freud still talks here of a *pre-sexual* stage and is therefore not fully aware of the fact that sexuality is an element of the child's personality from earliest infancy. In his letters to Fliess at this time there is evidence of Freud's reluctance to admit to himself the truth of what he was in the process of discovering, and which was so alien to the contemporary belief, hitherto shared by him, in the innocence of childhood.

In letters written in October and November 1895 Freud stated that he thought the secret he had confided to his friend could be regarded as a scientific fact, and from this he gained tremendous confidence and satisfaction:

> 16 October 1895 . . . I am practically sure I have solved the riddle of hysteria and obsessional neurosis with the formula of infantile sexual shock and sexual pleasure, and I am just as sure that both neuroses are radically curable now — not just the individual symptoms but the neurotic disposition itself. That gives me a kind of flat satisfaction — at having lived some forty years not quite in vain. (Ibid., p. 128)

And:

> 2 November 1895 . . . Today I am able to add that one of the two cases has given me what I was waiting for (sexual shock,

i.e., infantile abuse in a case of male hysteria!) and at the same
time some further working through the doubtful material has
strengthened my confidence in the correctness of my psychological assumptions. (Ibid., p. 132)

But two years later, on 21 September 1897, Freud confided
another much less cheering secret to his friend: he no longer
believed in his psychological hypothesis and he proceeded to
explain why this was so. Freud was compelled to refute his
own theories as a result of reassessing the clinical cases
themselves. Once again he was interested in the exception to
the rule, the one factor for which a new scientific hypothesis
could not account. This one factor led him on to further
hypotheses and to a realignment of the co-ordinates of his
research, even though this necessitated contradicting himself
and renouncing his newly acquired reputation as a great
healer with all the practical advantages this involved: 'The
hope of eternal fame was so beautiful, and so was that of
certain wealth, complete independence, travel and removing
the children from the sphere of worries which spoiled my
own youth. All that depended on whether hypnosis succeeded
or not' (ibid., pp. 217– 18).

Yet Freud was not 'depressed, jaded, unclear in [his] mind'.
He realized that his doubts were the result of 'honest and
effective intellectual labour, and [he was] proud that after
penetrating so far [he was] still capable of such criticism . . .
Can these doubts be only an episode on the way to further
knowledge?' (ibid., p. 217).

Freud enumerated these doubts, which were to be so rich
in positive consequences:

Even when patients were able to discover the early
'memory' of a sexual trauma they had experienced,
analysis failed to reach a positive conclusion.
It was hardly credible that perverted acts by adults on little

children should be as common as the frequency of
hysteria would lead one to suppose.

In the unconscious there is no hard and fast distinction
between real events and emotionally charged fiction.
However, one thing was certain: whether fact or fantasy,
sexual fantasy makes regular use of the theme of the
parents.

This last statement is very important from two points of
view. (1) If during analysis adult hysterics refer to childhood
seductions as having actually occurred when they are only
fantasies, then it is necessary to admit that the instincts and
desires responsible for such fantasies must exist. In other
words, *there exists in young children an autonomous sexuality
whose object is the parents*, and which has nothing to do with
seduction by adults. (This idea led to the Oedipus complex.)
(2) If analysis reveals the existence of instinctual urges in the
patient which other urges oppose by means of repression,
then the psyche must be composed of conflicting elements.
(This idea led to the distinction within the psyche between
the instinctual urges and the regulating forces.)

Self-analysis

At the same time Freud was investigating fantasies and
dreams whose irrationality particularly appealed to his rational
mind, and this work had an equal impact on the future of
psychoanalysis.

There are many references to the role and function of
fantasy or day-dreaming in the memos and letters which
Freud sent to Fliess to keep him abreast of his work. Like
dreams, these are the realization of a desire, or a compromise
between certain things which a person has seen or heard and
which have made an emotional impact on him.

As for dreams, we know that Freud's interest in psychic phenomena dated from the first years of clinical practice. In a note in the margin of Emmy von N.'s case history in 1889 there is a reference to the possibility of interpreting the apparent nonsense and inconsequentiality of dreams when they are spontaneously included in a patient's free association. We also know that from 1895 Freud began work on the material of dreams, referring frequently to the latter in his letters to Fliess and often giving interpretations of them. He refers to this work in the last chapter of *Project for a Scientific Psychology* (1895). This text, which was a project for a general approach to psychology based on neurology, was abandoned and only published posthumously in 1950. However, Freud did not abandon his ideas about the formation and meaning of dreams, and he later developed them in *The Interpretation of Dreams* (1900).

Freud's preoccupation with his own dreams and his attempts to interpret them which he reported to Fliess were a decisive factor in his progress from error (the theory of an infantile sexual trauma) to explanation (the theory of an autonomous infantile sexuality).

The study of his own dreams and fantasies was part of a wider process which occupied Freud during these years: he began to explore his own unconscious in the summer of 1897, shortly before writing his crucial letter of doubt to Fliess. There were a number of reasons which led Freud to embark on this task. He had written 15 years before: 'I always find it uncanny when I can't understand someone in terms of myself' (quoted by Jones in *The Life and Works of Sigmund Freud*, p. 277). He considered it vital for his clinical work that he should understand his own unconscious. But there were other, more personal reasons: the death of Freud's father in October 1897, apart from being a severe blow, revived Freud's former feelings for him.

It was precisely by analysing his previous feelings, the way they appeared to him in his dreams and the things with which they were associated that Freud was able to transmute the theory of infantile sexual trauma into that of infantile sexual instinct.

The Oedipus complex

Only a few days after writing to Fliess to tell him of his doubts concerning his theories about infant sexual trauma, Freud wrote to him again:

> 3 October 1897 . . . For the last four days my self-analysis, which I regard as indispensable for clearing up the whole problem, has been making progress in dreams and yielding the most valuable conclusions and evidence. (*Letters*, p. 218)

The most interesting of these conclusions from our point of view was that Freud had realized that his father was not the 'primary originator' of neurosis but that 'between the ages of two and two-and-a-half libido towards *matrem* was aroused; the occasion must have been the journey with her from Leipzig to Vienna, during which we spent a night together and I must have had the opportunity of seeing her *nudam*' (ibid., p. 219). Thus it was the infant Freud's precocious sexuality and not an act of adult seduction that was responsible for his sexual fantasies and memories. The extent to which the discovery disturbed him can be gauged by his use of Latin terms such as *matrem* and *nudam* in an attempt to lend an air of academic severity to an intimate confession.

In a later letter to Fliess Freud described the full impact of the sexual instinct on the infant psyche, and the complex network of its conflicting feelings towards the parents. In a letter to Fliess dated 15 October 1897 he described how, as a result of the systematic analysis of his own dreams, memories and associations, an idea of universal significance had emerged which was applicable to the individual human being in that it could explain not just his own behaviour but the extreme frequency of these 'sexual fantasies centring on the parents' which he had found in his adult patients as he delved further and further into their past. This idea is what came to be known as 'the Oedipus complex', that is to say, the interplay in the child's psyche of conflicting feelings derived from sexual instincts that exist independently in the child and are not intentionally encouraged by the adult.

The letter begins: 'My self-analysis is the most important thing I have in hand, and promises to be of the greatest value to me, when it is finished.' Then, after a detailed analysis of a dream about an old nurse, he assures Fliess that he will refer everything concerning his self-analysis to him systematically since 'being honest with oneself is a good exercise', and he finally gives the following account of his universally significant idea:

> I have found love of the mother and jealousy of the father in my own case too, and now believe it to be a general phenomen of early childhood, even if it does not always occur so early as in children who have been made hysterics . . . If that is the case, the gripping power of *Oedipus Rex*, in spite of all the rational objections to the inexorable fate that the story presupposes, becomes intelligible, and one can understand why later fate dramas were such failures. Our feelings rise against any arbitrary, individual fate . . . but the Greek myth seizes on a compulsion which everyone recognizes because he has felt traces of it in himself. Every member of the audience was once a budding Oedipus in phantasy, and this dream-fulfilment played out in reality causes everyone to recoil in horror, with the full measure of repression which separates his infantile from his present state. (Ibid., pp. 223—4)

He goes on to say that Shakespeare's Hamlet could be interpreted in the same way, in that the author's unconscious might be expressed in that of the hero. Hamlet's hesitation about avenging his father by killing his uncle ('Thus conscience doth make cowards of us all') stems from the anguish he feels at the obscure memory he had of himself meditating on committing the same deed on his father out of love for his mother. ('Use every man after his desert and who should 'scape whipping?') His conscience is his unconscious feeling of guilt.

Freud dealt with these examples in greater detail in *The Interpretation of Dreams* on which he was then working, and he included them in a chapter on 'Typical Dreams', that is, dreams which occur to almost everyone and which we may thus assume to have the same significance for all. Under this heading one finds dreams whose theme is the death of a parent, usually the parent of the same sex as the dreamer. These dreams are common among children aged three and over and they reveal quite explicitly the wish to eliminate the rival parent. Thus King Oedipus, who kills Laos his father and marries Jocasta his mother, presents us with the satisfaction of our childhood wish already realized and punished. In *Oedipus* the childhood fantasy or desire on which it is based is brought to the surface as in our own dreams. In *Hamlet* it remains repressed and we only become aware of its existence — as in the case of a neurotic person — through its inhibiting consequences.

Freud substantiated his theory by examining the dreams of his patients and of children, and by studying the latters' own straightforward and innocent comments. The myths and legends of primitive societies illustrate the same tragic rivalry between fathers and sons: Chronos devours his sons; Zeus emasculates his father and takes his place as ruler.

In 1900, three years after this letter to Fliess, the wealth of material which Freud had gathered led him to conclude:

> In my experience, which is already extensive, the chief part in
> the mental lives of children who later become psychoneurotics

is played by their parents. Being in love with the one parent and hating the other are among the essential constituents of the stock of psychical impulses which is formed at that time and which is of such importance in determining the symptoms of the later neurosis. It is not my belief, however, that psychoneurotics differ sharply in this respect from other human beings who remain normal — that they are able, that is, to create something absolutely new and peculiar to themselves. It is far more probable — and this is confirmed by occasional observations on normal children — that they are only distinguished by exhibiting on a magnified scale feelings of love and hatred for their parents which occur less obviously and less intensely in the minds of most children. (*The Interpretation of Dreams*, standard edn, vol. IV, pp. 260—1)

So the Oedipus complex is an obligatory stage in human development, but it becomes particularly intense within the nuclear family as described in chapter 1, in which the strict division of responsibilities between the mother who is in charge of the child's physical and personal well-being and the father who is the sole representative of the *potestas patris familias,* fosters the growth of the natural antagonism inherent in such relationships. The seed of this antagonism lies in the child's erotic feelings for the parent of the opposite sex and the tangle of ambivalent love—hate emotions the other parent arouses.

The notion of the Oedipus complex which is now an accepted part of contemporary culture caused such violent controversy in Freud's day that he saw the supporters and detractors of psychoanalysis itself in terms of people who accepted or refuted it.

Why is the Oedipus complex of such crucial importance? In chapter 1 we referred to the revolutionary impact it made from an historico-sociological standpoint; it implied the acknowledgement of autonomous infantile sexuality and thus the refutation of the myth of childhood innocence, and it weakened the sacred character of family order which Freud's contemporaries thought marked the height of cultural progress. But it had more important consequences in constituting the first step towards a study of cultural matters beyond the bounds of mere clinical case histories.

Our instinctive horror of incest, which Freud interpreted as a defence against incestuous infantile impulses which are so strong that they require an equally strong prohibition, drew his attention to those primitive societies where this horror is even more violently expressed than in civilized societies. In this way a new field of research was grafted on to clinical research: an anthropological study of myth and folklore. Chronologically the first of these studies was *Totem and Taboo* (1912–13). As Freud says in *An Autobiographical Study*: 'My starting-point was the striking correspondence between the two taboo-injunctions of totemism (not to kill the totem and not to have sexual relations with any woman of the same totem-clan) and the two elements of the Oedipus complex (killing the father and taking the other to wife)' (standard edn, vol. XX, p. 67).

The Oedipus complex marks a crucial stage in the psycho-sexual development of the individual — it is in fact the stage at which a normal or pathological development is determined. 'The Oedipus complex is the nodal complex of neurosis' according to Freud himself. This often misunderstood statement does not imply that the Oedipus complex is in itself the cause of neuroses: it is the failure to resolve this complex satisfactorily which can be pathogenic.

A mother would probably be horrified if she were made aware that all her marks of affection were rousing her child's sexual instinct and preparing for its later intensity. She regards what she does as asexual, 'pure' love, since, after all, she carefully avoids applying more excitations to the child's genitals than are unavoidable in nursery care. As we know, however, the sexual instinct is not aroused only by direct excitation of the genital zone. What we call affection will unfailingly show its effects one day on the genital zones as well. Moreover, if the mother understood more of the high importance of the part played by instincts in mental life as a whole — in all its ethical and psychical achievements — she would spare herself any self-reproaches even after her enlightenment. She is only fulfilling her task in teaching the child to love. After all, he is meant to grow up into a strong and capable person with vigorous sexual needs and to accomplish during his life all the things that human beings are urged to do by their instincts. (*Three Essays on the Theory of Sexuality*, standard edn, vol. VII, p. 223)

The importance of the Oedipus complex lies in the fact that the infantile sexual experience lays the foundations for the individual's future sexual life, and determines the adult's sexual normality, deviations, or fixations.

Freud discussed every possible implication of this concept in his writings. He described what might hypothetically be seen as the *positive* development of sexuality as well as its pathological developments: starting from the Oedipus complex he explained the process of its formation, the ways in which it differed for boys and girls and how it might be resolved. He saw the persistence of unresolved traces of this complex in the adult unconscious as the possible source of neurosis; and he studied the infinite complexities of the human condition which stem from this crucial point at which the individual's instinctual world first encounters his environment.

Freud's concern with the Oedipus complex and its consequence is reflected in all his work from this point on. In *Three Essays on the Theory of Sexuality* (1905) he traces the evolution of the sexual instinct from early infancy to puberty; and in *Contributions to the Psychology of Love* (1910–18) he explains how some types of male impotence and certain neurotic behaviour can be traced to an unresolved Oedipus complex in the unconscious. In *The Ego and the Id* (1923) he shows how the Oedipus complex is resolved and gives place to identification with the loved-hated parent; and how the resolution of the Oedipus complex leads to further complications if one takes into account the bisexuality of the individual. Finally, in 'The Dissolution of the Oedipus Complex' (1924) Freud explains how and why the Oedipus complex is resolved in boys and girls during the latency period.

Other essays deal more specifically with the role of the Oedipus complex in female sexuality and with the part it plays in the development of certain psychological characteristics peculiar to this sex — for instance: 'Some Psychical Consequences of the Anatomical Distinction between the Sexes' (1925), 'Female Sexuality' (1931) and 'Femininity' (1932). These texts develop at a theoretical level an enormous number of clinical experiences explored in their unconscious signification.

Chronology

1895   16 October: Letter to Fliess announcing his 'certainty' about childhood sexual trauma.

1897   Letter to Fliess announcing that he had ceased to believe in this hypothesis.

Summer: The start of Freud's self-analysis.

15 October: Letter to Fliess announcing his discovery of the Oedipus complex.

7

The Book of Dreams

What are dreams?

Freud began his self-analysis in August 1897. Through the systematic analysis of his own dreams he came to recognize his own childhood sexuality and thus formulated his general theory of infantile sexuality. Dreams therefore represented for Freud the 'key' to the world of impulses and desires which constitute the fundamental personality of an individual, and by analysing his own dreams and those of his patients he was able to formulate a theory of the interpretation of dreams which was of general psychological interest also, since it shed light on the workings of the psyche.

Freud defined dreams as: *the hallucinatory realizations of repressed desires.* In very young children this is quite evident: for instance, a three-year-old girl who had been put on a strict diet dreamed that she was eating as much as she wanted of all the things she was forbidden to eat — that is, she translated the forbidden act through which the *desire* was realized into a series of *images* (hence the term 'hallucinatory'). This dream is easy to interpret because the child's desire is clearly fulfilled in the dream scene. The child can go on sleeping while satisfying her desire and silencing the disturbing stimulus of her longing for food. The dream carries out its function as the guardian of sleep.

Adults' dreams are not so simple. The imaginary scene no longer translates the dreamer's desires literally: between the former (which Freud calls the *manifest content*) and the latter (which he calls the *latent content*) there is a notable discrepancy; the manifest content is a *distortion* of the latent content, and this distortion is achieved by the *dreamwork* which a specific psychic mechanism carries out according to specific rules.

The interpretation of dreams consists in proceeding from the manifest to the latent content by tracing the dream process in reverse order. In other words, the manifest content serves as a stimulus to the process of association. The association of thoughts, fantasies and memories may have no connection with the contents of the dream and may even seem meaningless and insignificant. But if thought is allowed to flow freely of any self-criticism (hence the term 'free association') an idea or a situation or a complex of situations emerges, charged with emotion and significance, and these are the driving forces of the dream.

The dreamwork

The process of distortion which turns the latent content of the dream into manifest content can be found in every person as a psychic activity that runs alongside the normal one but follows rules that do not apply to the waking mind. We shall mention only the most important.

Condensation

When we pass from the manifest to the latent content of a dream during the interpretative process we see that associative threads diverge in various directions from each element of the manifest content and lead to different impressions and events;

in other words the dream process condenses a number of emotive situations into a single image:

> Each element in the content of a dream is 'overdetermined' by material in the dream thoughts; it is not derived from a *single* element in the dream thoughts, but may be traced back to a whole number. These elements need not necessarily be closely related to each other in the dream thoughts themselves; they may belong to the most widely separated regions of the fabric of those thoughts. A dream element is, in the strictest sense of the word, the 'representative' of all this disparate material in the content of the dream. (*On Dreams*, standard edn, vol. V, p. 652)

A dream is thus a 'condensed substitute' for a set of thoughts charged with emotion and significance. It is as if this condensation were an attempt to give prominence to an element common to a combination of objects or images, by means of an ingenious abbreviation.

This process can be effected through a word with different possible interpretations, or through a composite image (for instance, of two people having something in common) — and it is this 'something' which the dream tries to bring to the fore. It may also be achieved by contrast: for instance, a patient called Mary dreamed that she was carrying a tall spray of flowers like those held by the angel in pictures of the Annunciation to represent innocence; but Mary's spray was of large white flowers like camellias, representing the very opposite of innocence by association with *La Dame aux Camélias* (ibid.).

Displacement

If condensation makes it difficult for non-specialists to decode a dream, another aspect of the dreamwork makes it even more so. This is the process of *displacement* by which, sometimes but not invariably, the apparently vague and insignificant elements in the dream form the main link with the dream thoughts or latent content, while the most vivid features are the least important. This is particularly true of dreams that appear incomprehensible precisely because the insignificant details are stressed, such as dreams in which the trivial events of everyday life seem to feature in a pointless way.

Freud observed that when these 'indifferent' dreams are analysed by the method of free association, their undoubtedly significant latent content is revealed, because 'dreams are never concerned with things with which we should not think it worth while to be concerned during the day, and trivialities which do not affect us during the day are unable to pursue us in sleep' (ibid., p. 656).

Symbolism

Dream symbolism is a further complication which has to be taken into account when interpreting dreams. A 'symbol' in the broad sense of the word signifies something that stands for something else. According to Freudian theory, certain images which are typical of the dreams of people belonging to the same linguistic or cultural group usually stand for something else, usually a repressed thought or desire, and the symbol by which these are expressed is the outer clothing which covers the desire. Freud believed that some symbols are of universal significance, and are to be found in the dreams of all individuals of all cultures, and also in fables, myths, legends and folklore. He therefore saw a close connection between dreams and the products of fantasy and art. On the other hand, this common identity would seem to suggest that symbolism is not peculiar to the dream process and has wider implications. The unconscious mind stores archaic images which reflect psychic activity from the earliest stages of human existence. The unconscious therefore not only represents the individual past but provides a link between ontogenesis and phylogenesis (or between the origins and the evolution of the species) — and with it the historical past of the whole human race. This is why the unconscious conflicts which are typical of human relationships have acquired names drawn from mythology where they are represented in a poetic guise. Having perceived the particular nature of dream symbols, Freud himself felt the need to link them with certain aspects of fable and folklore.

But each individual also creates certain symbols from his own store of imagery, and these are of a personal and well-defined nature.

It is therefore impossible to assume that dreams can be interpreted by the mechanical translation of a symbol into its corresponding significance. It is necessary to examine the ideas and images associated with a symbol, to take into account the circumstances in which the dream is told, the dreamer's behaviour before and after the analysis of the dream, and everything he reveals or hints at during his account of the dream, that is, during the same analytic session (see 'An evidential dream', 1913).

None the less, Freud gives an indication of the symbolic significance of certain recurrent dream images. A number of these have a sexual significance which concurs with Freud's theories of dream interpretation, for no other impulse has been as thoroughly repressed since childhood as the sexual impulse and so no other has left so many violently repressed desires in the unconscious which are revived during sleep and give rise to dreams. Once again Freud is led to attribute a fundamental importance to sexual instinct as a result of his clinical research, because it is through this that the repressed elements are reached. We have seen (chapter 1) how society in the time of Freud, precisely because of its particular characteristics, produced a situation in which a diffuse eroticism conflicted with the iron rules of behaviour that led to a rigid morality. It is thus the existential state of Freud's patients which 'compels' Freud to attach a fundamental value to the suppression of sexuality as the begetter of neuroses on one hand, and as the moving force of many dreams on the other. However, Freud always defends himself energetically against the accusation that, according to him, *all* dreams require a sexual interpretation. This assertion is alien to the fundamental thesis of *The Interpretation of Dreams*.

The language of the unconscious

We have discussed the condensation and displacement of images which can occur simultaneously in dreams, and also the use of symbols in dreams, but there is another process unique to dreaming and that is the translation into images of the logical links between two thoughts. The laws governing the functioning of the unconscious state began to absorb Freud's interest while he was writing his book on dreams, and took him beyond the original scope of the work.

We know that the waking mind is regulated by logical rules such as the law of opposites — that the opposite of true is false; the law of no third alternative — if you have two conflicting statements, one is true and one is false; the law of identity — that $a = a$; the law of cause and effect — that nothing happens without a cause or reason. In the unconscious mind these norms or laws are cancelled out or inverted or translated in terms of an individual's own imagery. For instance, a logical connection is replaced by the simultaneous occurrence in time and space of both elements. The causal relationship is replaced by a sequence of two strands of a dream — often the first stands for the result and the second for the cause. The alternative 'either/or' is replaced in the dream by 'and/and' — the dream includes both terms and gives them equal significance in the same context. The same image can express itself or its opposite. As we have seen, resemblance, similarity and common identity are dealt with by the process of *condensation* which reduces the various elements of emotive situations and images to a new single image.

Thus the unconscious speaks its own specific language and has its own particular 'syntax' which it uses both to reveal and to conceal in dreams; it has a different psychic activity from normal activity, is a characteristic of every human being and emerges during sleep, and it takes no account of the *reality principle*. In other words, it ignores the demands of the outside world and the need for the individual to restrain his instincts accordingly; indeed it acts wholly according to the *pleasure principle* at its most primitive and uncouth, that is, charged with emotive violence, and with no regard for the moral principles which are doubtless part of the dreamer's conscious personality. Freud called this part of the psychic process the *primary process,* as opposed to the *secondary process* which is governed by the logic of the waking mind.

The motives for dream distortion

'Dream thoughts', or the desires from which the dream stems, are not openly expressed in the manifest content and have to be interpreted before the muddled thread can be disentangled. But Freud wanted to find out the *motive* for this distortion.

> Our hypothesis is that in our mental apparatus there are two thought-constructing agencies, of which the second enjoys the privilege of having free access to consciousness for its products, whereas the activity of the first is in itself uncon-scious and can only reach consciousness by way of the second. On the frontier between the two agencies, where the

first passes over to the second, there is a censorship, which only allows what is agreeable to it to pass through and holds back everything else. According to our definition, then, what is rejected by the censorship is in a state of repression. Under certain conditions, of which the state of sleep is one, the relation between the strength of the two agencies is modified in such a way that what is repressed can no longer be held back. In the state of sleep this probably occurs owing to a relaxation of the censorship; when this happens it becomes possible for what has hitherto been repressed to make a path for itself to consciousness. Since, however, the censorship is never completely eliminated but merely reduced, the repressed material must submit to certain alterations which mitigate its offensive features. What becomes conscious in such cases is a compromise between the intentions of one agency and the demands of the other. *Repression — relaxation of the censorship — the formation of a compromise,* this is the fundamental pattern for the generation not only of dreams but of many other psychopathological structures; and in the latter cases, too, we may observe that the formation of compromises is accompanied by the processes of condensation and displacement and by the employment of superficial associations, which we have become familiar with in the dream work.

We have no reason to disguise the fact that in the hypothesis which we have set up in order to explain the dream work a part is played by what might be described as a 'demonic' element. We have gathered an impression that the formation of obscure dreams occurs *as though* one person who was dependent upon a second person had to make a remark which was bound to be disagreeable in the ears of this second one; and it is on the basis of this simile that we have arrived at the concepts of dream distortion and censorship, and have endeavoured to translate our impression into a psychological theory which is no doubt crude but is at least lucid. (*On Dreams,* standard edn, vol. V, pp. 676—7)

Freud's reference to 'demonism' recalls the medical and literary world's obsession at that very time with 'doubles', 'dual personalities' and the strange phenomena experienced by patients under hypnosis (see chapter 1). This mysterious 'double', existing alongside the self and interfering with its actions, is none other than a manifestation of the repressed material's evasion of censorship and emergence into the conscious mind: 'It will be seen that dreams are constructed like neurotic symptoms: they are compromises between the demands of a repressed impulse and the resistance of a censoring force in the ego. Since they have a similar origin they are equally unintelligible and stand in equal need of interpretation' (*An Autobiographical Study*, standard edn, vol. XX, p. 45). On the other hand, dreams are not in themselves pathological phenomena but phenomena of the normal psychic activity of any sane person:

> A dream, however, is no pathological phenomenon; it presupposes no disturbance of psychical equilibrium; it leaves behind it no loss of efficiency . . . . If, then, we may argue back from the phenomena to their motive forces, we must recognize that the psychical mechanism employed by neuroses is not created by the impact of a pathological disturbance upon the mind but is present already in the normal structure of the mental apparatus. The two psychical systems, the censorship upon the passage from one of them to the other, the inhibition and overlaying of one activity by the other, the relation of both of them to consciousness . . . all of these form part of the normal structure of our mental instrument, and dreams show us one of the paths leading to an understanding of its structure. (*The Interpretation of Dreams*, standard edn, vol. V, p. 607)

The crucial importance of *The Interpretation of Dreams* lies not only in its elucidation of the meaning of dreams, but in the recognition of the process of dream formation as a model for the processes which occur in the deepest layers of the psyche. As Freud was to declare:

what constitutes the enormous importance of dream interpretation, as well as of this latter study [*The Psychopathology of Everyday Life*], is not the assistance they give to the work of analysis but another of their qualities. Previously psychoanalysis had only been concerned with solving pathological phenomena and in order to explain them it had often been driven into making assumptions whose comprehensiveness was out of all proportion to the importance of the actual material under consideration. But when it came to dreams, it was no longer dealing with a pathological system, but with a phenomenon of normal mental life which might occur in any healthy person. If dreams turned out to be constructed like symptoms, if their explanation required the same assumptions — the repression of impulses, substitute-formation, compromise-formation, the dividing of conscious and unconscious into various psychical systems — then psychoanalysis was no longer a subsidiary science in the field of psycho-pathology, it was rather the foundation for a new and deeper science of the mind which would be equally indispensable for the understanding of the normal. Its postulates and findings could be carried over to other regions of mental happenings; a path lay open to it that led far afield into spheres of universal interest. (*An Autobiographical Study*, vol. XX, p. 47)

Thus Freud's book on dreams is of an exceedingly complex character:

It is the book in which Freud published the results of his self-analysis, and can thus be seen as an autobiography in depth.

In it, as well as analysing his own dreams, Freud analyses his patients' dreams, thus stipulating the basic condition for the formation of a therapeutic psychoanalytical relationship (only through a profound knowledge of oneself can one achieve an understanding of others).

It is a book about dreams, their function, their structure and their language.

But since this language is that of the unconscious — of a part of the psyche common to us all — it is also a book on general psychology which illustrates the particular way in which that part of the psyche expresses itself, and is linked with the other part we call consciousness.

It is a book which paves the way for research into other phenomena that are part of normal psychology but which none the less owe something to the unconscious: normal slips of the tongue, everyday omissions, over-sights, the mechanisms of wit and even artistic creation are partly indebted to an activity which is different from normal activity yet is intricately bound up with it.

Since the symbolic images of dreams use the same reper-tory as fables, myths and folklore, the 'archaic' is open to analysis also. It is a book in which by accepting the dream process as a paradigm for other normal and pathological psychic processes, Freud was 'compelled', as he put it, to postulate a model of the workings of the psyche which produce such phenomena.

Chronology

1900   Publication of *The Interpretation of Dreams.*
1901   Publication of *On Dreams,* a summary of *The Interpretation* aimed at a less specialized audience.
        Publication of *The Psychopathology of Everyday Life.*
        First draft of 'Fragment of an Analysis of a Case of Hysteria (Dora)', the original title of which was 'Dreams and Hysteria' and which was not published until 1905. This was in fact a sequel to *The Interpretation* in the field of clinical investi-gation.

8

The Workings of the Psyche

First outlines of a Freudian metapsychology

In the last chapter of *The Interpretation of Dreams* Freud expounded his theories on the functioning of the human psyche as deduced from his study of dreams. These theories constitute a first draft of the metapsychology which underpins psychoanalysis. 'These ideas are not the basis of the science upon which everything rests: that, on the contrary is observation alone. They are not the foundation-stone, but the coping of the whole structure, and they can be replaced and discarded without damaging it' ('On narcissism', standard edn, vol. XIV, p. 77).

Freud's working method was always one of cross-reference from clinical experience to theory and back to clinical experience, so his theories were in a constant state of evolution to include new experimental data the significance of which was clarified by the theories which were gradually taking shape.

This first 'model of the functioning of the human psyche' was strictly psychological and owed nothing to anatomical or physiological data (as had been the case in his 'Project for a Scientific Psychology' of 1895). Freud worked on his metapsychological theory throughout most of his life. In *The Ego and the Id* of 1923 he arrived at a synthesized systemization of the ideas included in earlier theoretical and clinical studies (such as *The Interpretation of Dreams* of 1900). *The Ego and the Id* is a seminal book to which to refer the reader who wishes to extend his knowledge of Freudian theory. It is also an extremely complex book and those who would like to gain an initial impression of the subject matter should consult *The Question of Lay Analysis* (1926) where Freud explains the workings of the psyche to an 'impartial' audience with no previous knowledge of psychoanalysis. It was written twenty-six years after the first outline in 1900 and yet even the last chapter of *The Interpretation of Dreams* contains the essence of Freud's thinking. We will therefore use the 1926 text here, referring to any important modifications made to the 1900 text.

Freud declares that he intends to expound his theory dogmatically, although it is in fact the outcome of a process which developed gradually according to his observations. Furthermore, he adds that he cannot guarantee that the terms he uses are definitely fixed and will not be modified again. He continues:

> We picture the unknown apparatus which serves the activities of the mind as being really like an instrument constructed of several parts (which we speak of as 'agencies'), each of which performs a particular function and which have a fixed spatial relation to one another: it being understood that by spatial relation — 'in front of' and 'behind', 'superficial' and 'deep' — we merely mean in the first instance a representation of the regular succession of the functions. (*The Question of Lay Analysis*, standard edn, vol. XX, p. 194)

By this Freud means that such 'spatial' demarcations are purely symbolic and have no anatomical connotations, such as 'zones of the brain'. He is merely trying to give a visual representation of the various functions of the psychic apparatus.

The ego occupies a central position in this, but what is the ego and what is its function? Freud writes: 'we recognize in human beings a mental organization which is interpolated between their sensory stimuli and the perception of their somatic needs on the one hand and their motor acts on the other, and which mediates between them for a particular purpose. We call this organization their "*Ich*" ["ego"; literally, "I"]' (ibid., pp. 194–5).[1] The ego's function is therefore to co-ordinate and mediate. But what does it co-ordinate and mediate and where does the material come from that is thus organized and mediated 'Besides this "I", we recognize another mental region, more extensive, more imposing and more obscure than the "I", and this we call the "Es" ["id"; literally "it"]' (ibid., p. 195). Freud considered that the impersonal pronoun *Es* (in English, 'It') was the most appropriate expression for the impersonal force by which we are lived while believing that it is we who do the living. He borrowed the term from his contemporary Groddeck, with whom he kept up an interesting correspondence.

> The ego . . . is the external, peripheral layer of the id. Now, we believe that on the outermost surface of this ego there is a special agency directed immediately to the external world, a system, an organ, through the excitation of which alone the phenomenon that we call consciousness comes about. This organ can be equally well excited from outside — thus receiving (with the help of the sense-organs) the stimuli from the external world — and from inside — thus becoming aware, first,

---

[1] We see here that the 'ego', that co-ordinating stage which serves as mediator, organizer and synthesizer, has assumed a far greater importance for Freud than it had in the first years when his interest was mainly centred on *impulses*. Freud's daughter Anna took it upon herself to examine in greater detail the numerous functions of this ego in its relation to the outer world and to the inner world of impulses. From 1922 Freud's interest in this subject deepened and he paved the way for the school of psychoanalytical studies known as Psychoanalytic Ego Psychology of which Hartmann is the most notable exponent.

of the sensations in the id, and then also of the processes in the ego. (Ibid., p. 198)

The ego and the id differ greatly from each other; different rules apply to each and the ego has different ends and different means. In *The Interpretation of Dreams* we came across the distinction between primary and secondary processes which influence what goes on at an unconscious level. For instance, the id knows no conflicts; contradictory terms and factors co-exist and indeed frequently combine in the form of compromises. The ego, on the other hand, cannot avoid conflicts and only solves them by renouncing one aim or urge in favour of another. The ego is characterized by a pronounced tendency to unify and synthesize, a feature the id entirely lacks, being as it were split so that its various tendencies pursue their independent ends regardless of each other. Everything that happens in the id is and remains unconscious. The processes of the ego can become conscious, but not all of them, and not all of the time, or invariably: large areas of the ego may remain permanently unconscious.

Here we note a discrepancy with what Freud had asserted in *The Interpretation of Dreams* where the ego and the conscious were one. This is an important modification resulting from Freud's clinical observations (for instance, the fact that the patient's resistance to analysis is obviously a part of the ego while also being unconscious). Thus *the unconscious* is no longer an exclusive quality of the id and of its content — every psychic stage is, to a certain extent, unconscious. This very important modification moved the focus of psycho-analysis from the id to the ego and to the 'super-ego', thereby extending the field of analytical investigation, and it simultaneously displaced the focus of therapy from the repressed material to the mode of repression, as we have noted.[2]

[2] For the concept of the *unconscious* see 'A Note on the Unconscious in Psycho-Analysis' (1912) and the first paragraph of *The Ego and the Id* (1923).

Returning to a description of the workings of the psyche we see that its inner functions are not restricted to the ego and the id. In *The Interpretation of Dreams* we came across the phenomenon of *censorship,* which is active in the dreamwork, where it creates distortions, but also in psychopathological cases where it produces symptoms. This censorship, which in *The Interpretation of Dreams* was ascribed to the ego, is really carried out by the 'super-ego':

> Within the ego itself a particular agency has become differentiated, which we name the super-ego. This super-ego occupies a special position betwen the ego and the id . . . It is in fact a precipitate of the first object-cathexes of the id and is the heir to the Oedipus complex after its demise. This super-ego can confront the ego and treat it like an object; and it often treats it very harshly. It is as important for the ego to remain on good terms with the super-ego as with the id . . . You will already have guessed that the super-ego is the vehicle of the phenomenon that we call conscience. (Ibid., p. 223)[3]

Thus apart from impulses which clamour for satisfaction, we are also subject to compulsions, prohibitions and aspirations which were once those of people whom, as children, we considered to be 'superior' and who are generally represented by our parents (in other words, *the first loves of the id*).

According to Freud, human beings thus find themselves in an awkward situation: the ego must mediate incessantly between the id, clamouring for instant satisfaction in response

---

[3] In part VII of *The Interpretation of Dreams,* standard edn, vol. V, pp. 557—60, on the subject of 'punishment dreams' Freud says that their essential character is that the dream-constructing wish is not an unconscious wish derived from the repressed material, but a punitive one reacting against it and belonging, although unconscious, to the ego. He adds in a footnote dated 1930: 'This would be the appropriate point for a reference to the "super-ego", one of the later findings of psychoanalysis.'

to the *pleasure principle,* and the outside world which stipulates the very different demands of the *reality principle.* Furthermore, it must also take into account the demands made on it by its own conscience or the 'super-ego'; in this way it is constantly engaged in a controversial battle on three fronts in its endeavour to achieve a satisfactory compromise.

This controversial situation is not in itself pathological — it is the human condition. Although it is obviously not easy to cope with, there is something stimulating and creative in the function of the ego as conciliator, mediator and co-ordinator. For the adult ego does not restrict itself to submitting to reality but usually discovers a means 'to intervene in the external world by *changing* it, and to establish in it intentionally the conditions which make satisfaction possible. This activity then becomes the ego's highest function' (ibid., p. 201).

Normality and neurosis

On the other hand, it is also a characteristic of the human condition that this difficult task can prove too much for us. If we consider that we must face it from our earliest years when the ego is still feeble and unstructured, it is easy to see how, in the process of setting up defences against inner impulses and adapting to the outside world, a child might opt for certain compromises which are not always satisfactory and resort to *pathogenic* solutions. Those solutions may be said to be pathogenic which, instead of giving the ego free access to the impulses — so that it can benefit from their energy while curbing them and giving them a satisfactory outlet — obstruct all access to the impulses, repressing them in the depths of the unconscious where they can no longer be put to any use.

The ego's quest for a satisfactory balance between the various aspects of the individual personality is frequently frustrated; and when this occurs the outcome is a *neurosis*. Its source may be found in earliest infancy at a time when the first conflicts with reality take place, although it may only manifest itself in various forms much later.

It may take the form of a state of *anxiety* which is the equivalent of an alarm signal, a warning of danger or of certain symptoms which the patient experiences as being foreign to his ego and which erupt against his will into his normal behaviour in a disturbing and unpleasant way; or again there may be neither anxiety nor symptoms, but the ego (that is, the individual's personality) fails to establish a satisfactory synthesis between his instinctual needs, the outside world and his own values, so that he behaves in an inhibited fashion, cannot pursue his aims, becomes lethargic and confused or excessively aggressive and tends, constantly, to make the wrong decisions.

The balance between the different elements of the human personality — the id, the ego with its mediating and co-ordinating functions and the 'super-ego' with its sense of values — and the outside influences with which these interact, can be disrupted or permanently impaired for a number of different but usually combined reasons. As a result of an exceptionally violent and impulsive nature, for instance, whether innate or caused by actual trauma, the ego's defences may have been destroyed. Or the defective ego may be seriously crippled or restricted by a rigid defence system, so that the impulses, which Freud compares to the energy propelling a steamship, are stifled to the extent that the ego is totally debilitated and exhausted. Or possibly the ego may have become inflexible in its strenuous resistance against the impulses which clamour for satisfaction, forcing it to expend all its energy in this way. The balance may also be impaired because of a pathological development in the conscience (or 'super-ego') which instead of guiding and directing behaviour, assumes the role of implacable and unconstructive

judge, submitting the ego to unrealistic demands and afflict-
ing it with a sense of guilt which is unrelated to any actual
misdeeds.

The above is obviously no more than a brief outline of the
various circumstances or sequence of circumstances which
can give rise to neuroses. It is important to note that Freud's
theory of the workings of the psyche as given in chapter VII
of *The Interpretation of Dreams* was subsequently amplified,
and as well as defining the ends and means of psychoanalytic
therapy, served as a basis for the study of normal and
pathological human behaviour. This behaviour is what manifests itself during analytic sessions in the relationship between
patient and analyst when the patient's particular resistances
and defences against his own impulses are re-enacted (as
opposed to remembered).

The psychotherapeutic investigation

What exactly does the psychoanalysis of human behaviour
involve?

The important factors to investigate are the impulses which
determine human behaviour, the resistance and restraints
applied by the ego and the 'super-ego', the ego's functions as
co-ordinator and mediator, and the impact exerted by reality.
An investigation of this nature considers the unconscious
factors which combine with the conscious ones to determine
our behaviour. These come to light through the process of
interpretation which works backwards from the influence
they have on known behaviour.

Freud rightly spoke of a new psychology, for by becoming
aware of the unconscious, by establishing the laws and the
syntax of the 'primary processes' and deciphering their
significance, he provides us with a much richer perspective

and deeper understanding of human nature and the problems
of existence. As Freud said in *The Ego and the Id*:

> The division of the psychical into what is conscious and what
> is unconscious is the fundamental premiss of psycho-analysis;
> and it alone makes it possible for psycho-analysis to under-
> stand the pathological processes in mental life, which are as
> common as they are important, and to find a place for them in
> the framework of science. To put it once more, in a different
> way: psycho-analysis cannot situate the essence of the psychical
> in consciousness, but is obliged to regard consciousness as a
> quality of the psychical which may be present in addition to
> other qualities or may be absent. (Standard edn, vol. XIX,
> p. 3)

The metapsychological perspectives revealed by the working
of the psyche enable one to define Freud's general therapeutic
aims. The analytic method endeavours to restore the ego, to
free it from its constraints and re-establish its authority over
the id which it had lost as a result of early repression. These
constraints emerge during therapy in the form of resistances,
that is, the patient re-enacts a certain pattern of behaviour
instead of remembering it. The analysis of this behaviour
pattern, with assistance from dreams and free association, will
lead to the first conflicts in the course of which these
constraints were first established, and from these to the first
impulses which determined them. At this stage, when the
patient becomes consciously aware of these constraints, his
defence mechanisms can be re-examined. Since infancy these
have served and still serve the purpose of keeping at bay
certain simultaneously internal and external dangers (for
instance, the satisfaction of an urge may have incurred
external punishment).

> It sometimes turns out that the ego has paid too high a price
> for the services they render it. The dynamic expenditure

necessary for maintaining them, and the restrictions of the ego which they almost invariably entail, prove a heavy burden on the psychical economy. Moreover, these mechanisms are not relinquished after they have assisted the ego during the difficult years of its development ... They become regular modes of reaction of his character, which are repeated through out his life whenever a situation occurs that is similar to the original one. This turns them into infantilisms, and they share the fate of so many institutions which attempt to keep themselves in existence after the time of their usefulness has passed. ('Analysis terminable and interminable', standard edn, vol. XXIII, p. 237)

Some of these may be eliminated, others made less potent, and those which are ego-syntonic, that is, consistent with the overall personality of the patient, may be strengthened. It is essential that the repressed desires should no longer be buried in the unconscious, but the patient should be made aware of them and they should be reintegrated within the synthesis of the ego.

Freud is not blind to the difficulties inherent in this approach to psychoanalytic therapy, in the risk of error and the sometimes insuperable obstacles that confront the would-be analyst. Nothing could be more remote from Freud's attitude than exultation, as is evident from his constant reworking of his discoveries and methods and constant awareness of their shortcomings. In 'Analysis Terminable and Interminable' he emphasizes these pitfalls when comparing theoretical with experimental data. Responding to a question as to whether analysis achieves its aims and whether it does so conclusively and invariably, his answer is a model of realism and prudence:

The effect brought about in the ego by the defences can rightly be described as an 'alteration of the ego' if by that we understand a deviation from the fiction of a normal ego which would guarantee unshakable loyalty to the work of analysis. It is easy, then, to accept the fact, shown by daily experience, that the outcome of an analytic treatment depends essentially on the strength and on the depth of root of these resistances that bring about an alteration of the ego. Once again we are confronted with the importance of the quantitative factor, and once again we are reminded that analysis can only draw upon definite and limited amounts of energy which have to be measured against the hostile forces. (Ibid., pp. 239—40)

And later in the same essay:

Our aim will not be to rub off every peculiarity of human character for the sake of a schematic 'normality', nor yet to demand that the person who has been 'thoroughly analysed' shall feel no passions and develop no internal conflicts. The business of the analysis is to secure the best possible psychological conditions for the functions of the ego; with that it has discharged its task. (Ibid., p. 250)

Analysis is therefore not considered to be a conclusive intervention; it should encourage the patient to conduct his own self-analysis on the strength of an improvement in the function of his ego, and to pursue the obviously interminable process of self-exploration.

Chronology

1899   3 January: Letter to Fliess announcing his latest discovery. 'It is dawning. In the next few days there will certainly be something to add . . . If I wait a little longer I shall be able to describe the mental process in dreams in such a way as to include the process in hysterical symptoms.'

January — September: He drafts chapter VII of *The Interpretation*.

11 September: Letter to Fliess. 'I have finished; that is to say the manuscript has gone off . . . As for the psychological part, I am leaving it to your judgement whether I should revise it again or let it go as it is. The matter about dreams I believe to be unassailable; what I dislike about it is the style. I was quite unable to express myself with noble simplicity.'

9

Three Essays on the Theory
of Sexuality

Sexual deviation

In the first chapter of this book we noted how and why it was so essential for the society in which Freud grew up to believe in the 'innocence' of children and in the image of the family as the stronghold which protected this innocence. Freud's discovery of infant sexuality, which he was prepared to recognize only after a tremendous struggle with his own prejudices, completely shattered the reassuring image of the nuclear family, and opened up the field of research into sexuality and its complex evolution from the earliest stages of infancy.

From 1897 to 1905 Freud gradually developed his theories about sexuality and published the results in *Three Essays on the Theory of Sexuality* (1905).

As noted earlier, Freud discovered the importance of the sexual factor through his clinical observations; he had no preconceived ideas on the subject. The first of the three essays therefore starts with a study of sexual aberrations in adults as he had observed them in his clinical practice. These aberrations, with which contemporary sexologists were perfectly familiar, were classified according to whether they deviated from what was seen as sexually normal. The object of someone's attentions, instead of being an adult of the opposite sex might be someone of the same sex, or a child or an animal;

sexual activity might not be directed towards normal intercourse but towards other parts of the body, or even towards
some object that served as a substitute, as in fetishism; or, as
in sadism, its aim might be to cause physical pain instead of
giving and receiving pleasure.

Deviations of this nature are not only found in people
suffering from severe mental illness; they can occur, as simple
sexual deviations, in otherwise normal people. We know,
moreover, that in certain cultures at certain times some
inversions (such as homosexuality) were considered normal
for people of a given age. According to Freud we will find
vestiges of deviated sexuality in what we consider to be
normal sexuality today. This is true of children's sexual
games, for instance, which commonly occur between individuals of the same sex; and of people in love who gain a
heightened pleasure from their partner's body as a whole, and
not just from the sexual organs (kissing and caressing, for
instance); or of a certain amount of aggressiveness which
comes into play in most men during sexual intercourse, or of
the total submission to the sexual partner, these attitudes
having overtones of sadistic or masochistic tendencies.

Sexual inclinations and desires dreamed about by neurotics
if not restrained by inhibitions would lead to deviant behaviour. When the neurotic symptoms are subjected to analysis
they prove to be a compromise in which the repressed desire
appears in a distorted form after being restrained by the
prohibitions imposed by the ego on what it deems unacceptable.

In the case of perverts, or those who, unlike neurotics,
actually activate their abnormal sexual instincts, it is the
unification of the various impulses under the genital primacy
which is impaired: a partial aim dominates the sexual drive
and thus hinders the development of normal sexuality. These
people should be seen as individuals who have remained

fixated at or have regressed to an infantile stage of sexual development, since it is in early childhood itself that sexuality is 'unfocused'. Freud drew an important conclusion from these considerations: 'We are thus warned to loosen the bonds that exist in our thoughts between instinct and object. It seems probable that the sexual instinct is in the first instance independent of its object' (*Three Essays on the Theory of Sexuality*, standard edn, vol. VII, p. 148).

Sexuality must be seen to have a much wider significance than it had hitherto been credited with. It is not only the attraction experienced at puberty for persons of the opposite sex as a consequence of the maturing of the sexual organs. It is an instinct which manifests itself in early childhood when it seeks pleasure with no predetermined object in view. Thus perversion seen as a quest for non-genitally oriented pleasure is potentially inherent in all human beings. The study of adult perversions provides a key to an understanding of infantile sexuality and the latter, in turn, enables us to explain perversions as cases of arrested development, or of sexual regression or fixation in the course of normal sexual development.

In the other two essays Freud studies the sexual impulses of children and traces their complex development as far as puberty, noting the various stages of their evolution.

Pre-genital infantile stages

These stages follow one after the other but even in normal development each successive stage preserves traces of previous ones; the adult genital stage — or that in which the individual gains pleasure from a complete sexual relationship with someone of the opposite sex — does not eliminate the other stages but includes them, the genital stage taking priority. The pleasures of the infantile stages persist as less important elements, or as elements preparatory to adult pleasure.

During the first stage, which occurs soon after birth, the child's instinct is *auto-erotic,* that is, he finds pleasure and satisfaction in his own body, especially in his mouth. This is the *oral stage*; the child's habit of sucking, even when not absorbing food, is a symptom of this kind of pleasure-seeking; and Freud defined it as sexual because, as we have seen, even though it has nothing to do with adult, or genital sexuality, it is none the less an erotic pleasure. After the oral stage comes the *anal stage* when pleasurable sensations are derived from the anus in retaining or expelling faeces. Later still — between the ages of three and five — comes the *phallic stage* when pleasure becomes centred on the genital region, on the penis in boys and the clitoris in girls.

It was not at first apparent to Freud that the phallic stage should be included in the pre-genital stages. In a footnote added to the *Three Essays* in 1924 he wrote:

> At a later date (1923), I myself modified this account by inserting a third phase in the development of childhood, subsequent to the two pre-genital organizations. This phase, which already deserves to be described as genital, presents a sexual object and some degree of convergence of the sexual impulses upon that object; but it is different from the final organization of sexual maturity in one essential respect. For it knows only one kind of genital: the male one. For that reason I have named it the 'phallic' stage of organization. (Ibid., p. 199n)

Here Freud introduces the concept of the individual's bisexuality during the first years of childhood. By this he means that each individual has both male and female tendencies — not of course anatomically but psychologically, that is, in the world of fantasies, images and desires. We shall see how this concept was to make Freud's account of normal sexual development richer and more complex. In the *Three Essays* he declared: 'Since I have become acquainted with the notion of bisexuality I have regarded it as the decisive factor, and without taking bisexuality into account I think it would scarcely be possible to arrive at an understanding of the sexual manifestations that are actually observed in men and women' (ibid., p. 220). We shall see later, however, that Freud's concept of 'femininity' never became sufficiently clear. In the meantime let us return to the development of the sexual instincts.

Relation to the object

Another angle from which to consider the development of sexuality is that of its relation to the object. In *Three Essays* Freud did not deal with the subject in depth; during the years that follows its publication he made essential modifications to his theories on the subject.

During the first months of life the child has as yet no images of objects, and the first images he perceives are blurred, so that the figure of his mother, or the person taking this role, has no clear outline. The child feels as it were fused and confused with his mother's body, and experiences a kind of omnipotence precisely because he is as yet unaware of the boundaries between himself and what is other than himself, and he imagines that the whole world, or at least part of it, is contained within him. This narcissistic stage is gradually modified by contact with reality. Little by little the child is able to perceive his mother as a distinct being, different from himself and different from anyone else. The child's attachment to his mother is the main characteristic of infant sexuality (until the age of three) and is common to boys and girls. Later (between the ages of three and five) the father appears on the scene as a simultaneously loved and disturbing object. This gives rise to that tangle of ambivalent feelings which has been called the Oedipus complex.

Thus the Oedipus complex and the emotive turmoil it involves coincides with an infantile sexual stage in which the mother is the object of the sexual fantasies of both boys and girls, but with different implications for each sex. For boys the Oedipus complex represents the climax of the first stage of infantile sexuality: the mother is the sexual object and the father the loved and dreaded rival. For girls the development is less simple. Before a girl can enter the Oedipal phase and concentrate on her father she has to abandon her first love-object, her mother. This, according to Freud, is achieved by renouncing the phallic posture (that is, focusing on the clitoris as a penis-substitute). There are various reasons why this happens, such as the pressures of education which are more primitive and repressive in relation to masturbation in the case of girls than in boys; but the main one is the discovery of sexual differentiation. When a little girl first sees the male genitals she tends to consider the lack of such an attribute as an impairment; she will hold her mother responsible for this and turn away from her towards her father.

In consequence, passive desires, such as conceiving a child by the father, will replace active ones, centred on the clitoris, in the fantasies of the female infant, and in this way she comes to accept her femininity.

It is thus the discovery of the difference between the sexes which initiates the Oedipus complex in girls. The discovery has the opposite effect on boys. We have seen that during the phallic stage their pleasurable sensations are derived from the genitals as an inevitable result of outside stimulation — accidentally in nursery care, or directly, since this is the age when masturbation is first practised. The mother is the object of the boy's fantasies: he wants somehow to replace his father, to eliminate him as a rival. On the other hand, his fear of being punished for this aggressive desire becomes a dread of castration, of being deprived of the male organ which has become such a valuable source of pleasure. It is his discovery of the female genitals which apparently lack his own attributes which suggest the notion of castration as punishment. As in the case of the little girl, threats may reinforce this fear, such as his mother or nurse saying they will cut off his hand or his penis if he is found masturbating, or even a distressing comparison with his father's so much more imposing penis. The main factor which will finally lead to the resolution of the boy's Oedipus complex is the fear of castration. According to Freud, 'whereas in boys the Oedipus complex is destroyed by the castration complex, in girls it is made possible and led up to by the castration complex' ('Some psychical consequences of the anatomical distinction between the sexes', standard edn, vol. XIX, p. 256). The way in which boys and girls resolve the complex is also different. A boy's jealousy of his father leads to identification.

> The girl's Oedipus complex ... seldom goes beyond the taking of her mother's place and the adopting of a feminine attitude towards her father. Renunciation of the penis is not tolerated by the girl without some attempt at compensation. She slips — along the line of a symbolic equation, one might say — from the penis to a baby. Her Oedipus complex culminates in a desire, which is long retained, to receive a baby from her father as a gift — to bear him a child. One has an impression that the Oedipus complex is then gradually given up because this wish is never fulfilled. ('The dissolution of the Oedipus complex', standard edn, vol. XIX, pp. 178–9)

And 'in her, far more than in the boy, these changes seem to be the result of upbringing and of intimidation from outside which threatens her with a loss of love'. Freud concludes this passage with an admission he frequently made on the subject of female sexuality: 'It must be admitted, however, that in general our insight into these developmental processes in girls is unsatisfactory, incomplete and vague' (ibid., p. 179).

Latency

After the first flowerings of infantile sexuality a *period of latency* usually occurs lasting from the age of five or six until puberty; during this period sexuality becomes dormant and, under the influence of education on the one hand and the passing of the Oedipus complex on the other, its activity is directed towards other than sexual ends. Moreover, mental barriers, such as modesty and disgust, are set up, and a moral and aesthetic sensibility is established which derive their strength from this diversion of sexuality. For instance, the flow of erotic feeling towards one or other parent is transformed into tender affection; the preoccupation with faeces and excremental functions turns into an obsession with personal cleanliness and tidiness as a means of expressing regard and love for those who are caring for the growing child. Social instincts are awakened by the child's association with other children and are expressed in a general compliance with certain principles and ideals; and the child's personality, which was already outlined in the early stages of sexuality, will become stronger.

In these early years the individual's character is formed as a sort of compromise between his instincts at various stages (oral, anal, phallic) and the influence of the mental barriers set up during the period of latency to channel and modify them.

If therefore a person remains fixated at the stage of *oral* sexuality — which corresponds to the time when the child begins to perceive his love-objects — his character will show signs of a certain passive dependence on others; or he may be excessively demanding and have an annoying tendency to exert a constant pressure on others to make sure of their respect or their love. If on the other hand, he is fixated at the anal stage he will be extremely tidy, parsimonious and stubborn on account of the defence mechanisms built up during his childhood against the desires and satisfactions corresponding to the anal period. Freud discusses this subject in his essay 'Character and Anal Eroticism'.

As in neurosis and 'normality', neither the oral nor the phallic element are of a pathological nature, since they represent normal phases in human development; it is the failure to find a balance between instinct and defence mechanism which creates *fixations* which may become pathological.

Freud's early observations in this field led to the development of a very interesting branch of research known as *psychoanalytic characterology*, which has both clinical and anthropological applications. W. Reich is one of its most prominent exponents.

Freud called the process of transformation which occurs during the period of latency *sublimation*, and he defined the mechanism as follows:

It is possible further to form some idea of the mechanism of this process of sublimation. On the one hand, it would seem, the sexual impulses cannot be utilized during these years of childhood, since the reproductive functions have been deferred — a fact which constitutes the main feature of the period of latency. On the other hand, these impulses would seem in themselves to be perverse — that is, to arise from erotogenic zones and to derive their activity from instincts which, in view of the direction of the subject's development, can only arouse unpleasurable feelings. They consequently evoke opposing mental forces (reacting impulses) which, in order to suppress this unpleasure effectively, build up the mental dams that I have already mentioned. (*Three Essays on the Theory of Sexuality*, standard edn, vol. VII, p. 178)

A sub-species of sublimation is *reaction formation,* or the powerful suppression of the sexual impulses which are expressed in actions and attitudes diametrically opposed to the impulses themselves; for instance, a reaction formation against anal erotic tendencies could take the form of a violent distaste for anything unclean; or, more generally, a powerful sexual instinct will be expressed in an ascetic detachment from all sensual pleasures, even those not directly related to sex.

Unlike sublimation, where the impulse can be satisfied by altering its original objective or by a process of de-sexualization (as when the child's erotic attraction to the parent of the opposite sex may be redirected to a different person who is not a member of the family, or be transformed into tender affection), reaction formation reverses the urge itself: this results in inflexible behaviour and a lack of spontaneity.

None the less, it is during the period of latency that the individual's character is formed, if character formation is to be seen as the organization of one's defences against one's instincts. This defence process encourages the formation of moral and social ideals by developing the super-ego and repressing the more primitive instincts:

> What we describe as a person's 'character' is built up to a considerable extent from the material of sexual excitations and is composed of instincts that have been fixed since childhood, of constructions achieved by means of sublimation, and of other constructions, employed for effectively holding in check perverse impulses which have been recognized as being unutilizable. The multifariously perverse sexual disposition of childhood can accordingly be regarded as source of a number of our virtues, insofar as . . . it stimulates their development. (Ibid., pp. 238—9)

At the end of the period of latency, between the ages of 12 and 13, the period of puberty begins, and, as a consequence of changes in the body, sexual instincts re-emerge in full force and significant modifications take place.

Changes at puberty

In physical terms puberty is characterized by the maturing of the external and internal genital organs; the male will have his first ejaculation, the female will begin to menstruate. Psychologically two notable changes occur:

> The genital zone takes precedence over all other erotogenic zones, which become mere preliminaries to the new sexual objective.
>
> In puberty, when the child's sexual inclinations reassert themselves, the choice of object, or sexual partner, is diverted away from the parent or parent substitute on which they focused in infancy to someone similar, as a result of the mental barrier formed during the latency period as a protection against incest.

During puberty the male's sexual 'history' becomes quite distinct from the female's: whereas the phallic sexual impulses of the former are directed towards women — that is, persons of the same sex as the original love-object — the latter has to change the 'directive zone' of her sexuality. As we know, during infancy girls derive sexual pleasure from masturbation of the clitoris, which corresponds to the boy's penis:

> If we are to understand how a little girl turns into a woman, we must follow the further vicissitudes of the excitability of the clitoris. Puberty, which brings about so great an accession of libido in boys, is marked in girls by a fresh wave of *repression*, in which it is precisely clitoridal sexuality that is

affected. What is thus overtaken by repression is a piece of masculine sexuality . . . When at last the sexual act is permitted and the clitoris itself becomes excited, it still retains a function: the task, namely, of transmitting the excitation to the adjacent female parts, just as — to use a simile — pine shavings can be kindled in order to set a log of harder wood on fire. Before this transference can be effected, a certain interval of time must often elapse, during which the young woman is anaesthetic. (Ibid., pp. 220—1)

Although this can be seen as the normal course of development, each step along this protracted evolutionary path may become a point of fixation, each stage in this complex progression a chance for the sexual impulses to become dissociated. In the *Three Essays* Freud describes the problems which arise when certain stages are not resolved satisfactorily: for instance, the adolescent may not be able to renounce the first infantile love-object, and this exaggerated affection may prove an obstacle in the later choice of a partner; or again, defences against sexuality may be strengthened leading to the inability to conceive of love as anything but 'pure', desexualized and totally devoid of the dreaded (though secretly desired) erotic element. Freud constantly stressed the link that exists between infantile and adult eroticism, and he contributed a number of important theories on the subject.

Fixation can also occur because of the nature of the impulse itself, and not just through the object of a person's choice. As we noted in the section on sexual deviation, each partial aim can become predominant, and fail to give that primacy to the genital which is necessary if full sexual satisfaction is to be achieved. We also noted that excessive repression may result in a kind of alienation of the impulse itself when it remains buried in the unconscious, manifesting itself later in the form of that compromise between impulse and defence mechanism which is the symptom of a neurosis.

A comment

During this period the individual's impulses, fantasies and emotions interact with external factors, that is, in his relationships with other people.

This brief account of the *Three Essays* gives little impression of their complexity and richness. The impression of 'normal' development which emerges from it is, like the term itself, too rigid to do justice to all Freud has to say on the subject. In the *Three Essays,* as in all his work on the problem of the evolution of the libido and its relationship with the outside world, Freud emphasizes that 'normality' and 'sanity' are abstract concepts since we never come across an individual in real life whose psyche does not bear the mark of the maturing process, of some perversion (some residue of the impulses belonging to one or other infantile stage) or neurosis (some not entirely successful repression). Writing many years later about the way in which the object — or sexual partner — is selected, that is, the formation and resolution of the Oedipus complex, Freud declared: 'I have no doubt that the chronological and causal relations described here between the Oedipus complex, sexual intimidation (the threat of castration), the formation of the super-ego and the beginning of the latency period are of a typical kind; but I do not wish to assert that this type is the only possible one' ('The dissolution of the Oedipus complex', standard edn, vol. XIX, p. 179).

The manner in which the Oedipus complex is formed and resolved in an individual is evidently influenced by external factors, for instance, the structure of the family and its particular social context, the relationship between the parents, the personality of each of the protagonists of this triangle, whether there are brothers and sisters or not, etc. The way in which the individual has lived through the pre-genital period, that is, during the years preceding the formation of the complex, is also an influencing factor. Nothing is further from Freud's intention than to give the impression that he could distil the infinite variety of human experience into a single comprehensive formula.

None the less, Freud's discovery of infantile sexuality remains irrefutable, as is his appreciation of its enormous significance in the development of the psyche and the complex relationships it establishes with its first love-objects, that is, with those people with whom the child comes into contact emotionally in his earliest years.

Freud's discovery of infantile bisexuality constitutes another permanent contribution to the sum of our knowledge of human nature. We have seen that during the phallic stage the characteristics of each sex are indistinct: the focus of interest for both boys and girls is the phallus (or male penis and female clitoris). Girls therefore have psychological characteristics of a masculine nature. But boys too experience tender, passive feelings for one parent and corresponding jealousy for the other. This bisexuality cannot fail to complicate the image of 'normality' in so far as each normal individual has both male and female elements in his make-up.

Freud clarified the conventional meanings of the terms 'masculine' and 'feminine' in a substantial note which he appended to the *Three Essays* in 1915:

> It is essential to understand clearly that the concepts of 'masculine' and 'feminine' whose meaning seems so unambiguous to ordinary people, are among the most confused that occur in science. It is possible to distinguish at least *three* uses. 'Masculine' and 'feminine' are used sometimes in the sense of *activity* and *passivity*, sometimes in a *biological*, and sometimes, again, in a *sociological* sense. The first of these three meanings is the essential one and the most serviceable in psychoanalysis. When, for instance, libido was described in the text above as being 'masculine', the word was being used

in this sense, for an instinct is always active even when it has a passive aim in view. The second, or biological, meaning of 'masculine' and 'feminine' is the one whose applicability can be determined most easily. Here 'masculine' and 'feminine' are characterized by the presence of spermatozoa or ova respectively and by the functions proceeding from them. Activity and its concomitant phenomena (more powerful muscular development, aggressiveness, greater intensity of libido) are as a rule linked with biological masculinity; but they are not necessarily so, for there are animal species in which these qualities are on the contrary assigned to the female. The third, or sociological, meaning, receives its connotation from the observation of actually existing masculine and feminine individuals. Such observation shows that in human beings pure masculinity or femininity is not to be found either in a psychological or in a biological sense. Every individual on the contrary displays a mixture of the characteristics belonging to his own and to the opposite sex; and he shows a combination of activity and passivity whether or not these last character traits tally with his biological ones. (Standard edn, vol. VII, p. 219n)

Freud refers again and again in his writings to the problematic and potentially ambiguous use of the terms 'masculinity' and 'femininity'. Sometimes, as in this footnote, he stressed their conventional meaning (that is, a meaning which does not seek to make masculine or feminine psychological traits fit the individual of male or female sex); at other times, however, he stressed the psychological distinction between the sexes until they appear to be two practically different 'psychic species', different precisely because of their biological distinctness.

As he himself was well aware, Freud was never able to encompass these different views in one comprehensive formula. In the *Three Essays* he admits that the development of masculine sexuality is more consistent and more easy to understand than that of feminine sexuality. In 1926 after many years of research into the problems of feminine sexuality he still spoke of it as unexplored or even undiscovered territory: 'We know less about the sexual life of little girls than of boys. But we need not feel ashamed of this distinction; after all, the sexual life of adult women is a "dark continent" for psychology' (*The Question of Lay Analysis,* standard edn, vol. XX, p. 212).

This is the least satisfactory area of Freud's work, as he himself was the first to admit. Its lack of solution gave rise to two schools of thought among Freud's opponents and followers. The first, known as the 'left wing', stems from Freud's theory but stresses the relative independence of the psychological from the biological, and thus denies the necessary existence of the above-mentioned characteristics in the female individual. The other, known as the 'right wing', tends on the contrary to accentuate their dependence. Even this school of thought could justifiably lay claim to a Freudian derivation, while ignoring, however, Freud's concept of human bisexuality and the decisive influence of the cultural background. At the end of an essay on femininity written in 1933 Freud wrote: 'I have promised to tell you a few more psychical peculiarities of mature femininity, as we come across them in analytic observation. We do not claim to more than an average validity for these assertions, nor is it always easy to distinguish what should be ascribed to the influence of the sexual function and what to social breeding' ('Femininity', in *New Introductory Lectures on Psycho-Analysis,* standard edn, vol. XXII, p. 132).

In his 1909 preface to the *Three Essays* Freud expressed the 'earnest wish that the book may age rapidly, that what was once new in it may become generally accepted, and what was imperfect in it may be replaced by something better'. That is indeed what has happened. Today the concept of infantile sexuality has lost its flavour of novelty, and it seems odd that people in Vienna and Europe as a whole, who were so interested in sex both socially and scientifically, should so violently oppose Freud and his theories on the subject. Freud's biographer Jones gives a detailed account of some of the adverse reactions which his theories provoked. We are told that when Spielmeyer first reviewed Freud's analysis of Dora, he described the method as 'mental masturbation'. Ashaffenburg, at a congress in Baden-Baden in May 1906, came to the conclusion that 'Freud's method is wrong in most cases, objectionable in many and superfluous in all'. Furthermore, it was immoral. In 1907 at a congress in Amsterdam, 'striking his breast with a gesture of self-righteousness, he asseverated how he forbade his patients ever to mention any sexual topic'. At the close of the congress Konrad Alt promised, amid great applause, 'that no patient of his should ever be allowed to reach any of Freud's followers with their conscienceless descent into absolute filth'. On 9 November 1908, during a discussion which followed the reading of a paper on the erotic aspects of consanguinity by Abraham before the Psychiatric Association, Bratz 'cried out that German ideals were at stake and that something drastic should be done to protect them'. In far-off Australia 'the Presbyterian clergyman Donald Fraser had to leave the ministry because of his sympathy with Freud's work'. In the same year (1908) Jones himself 'was forced to resign a neurological appointment in London for making inquiries into the sex life of patients'. At a congress of German neurologists and psychiatrists in Hamburg (1910) Professor Weygandt shouted: 'this is not a topic for discussion at a scientific meeting; it is a matter for the police'. And in the same year at the Neurological Congress of Berlin Professor Oppenheim 'proposed a boycott to be established of any institution where Freud's views were tolerated' (*The Life and Works of Sigmund Freud*, pp. 381−5).

The indignation of Freud's contemporaries had nothing to

do with the fact that as a scientist he was interested in sexuality and its deviations; what they could not accept was that sexuality was a feature of childhood, where it was naturally perverse — that is, not genitally orientated, that its first object was a parent and, above all, that it was present in this *abnormal* form in all *normal* people. Equally scandalous or perhaps more so was Freud's theory relating to the period of latency, according to which the generally perverse dispositions of infancy become the source of many of our virtues in that they provide the energy from which these spring.

This theory was far removed from the ideology of the period and its vision of the 'upright man', free, through the integrity of his noble nature, from the vices harboured by the degenerate; if the 'upright man' was at all affected by these, it was thought to be the work of external forces of corruption, or even influences of a diabolical nature.

According to Freud:

Historians of civilization appear to be at one in assuming that powerful components are acquired for every kind of cultural achievement by the diversion of sexual instinctual forces from sexual aims and their direction to new ones — a process which deserves the name of 'sublimation'. To this we should add, accordingly, that the same process plays a part in the development of the individual and we would place its beginning in the period of sexual latency of childhood. (*Three Essays on the Theory of Sexuality*, standard edn, vol. VII, p. 178)

On the one hand Freud stressed the importance of sexual instincts, thereby arousing the wrath of those who consider that instinctual forces derived from organic needs are damaging to the forces which create moral and social values and should therefore be energetically repressed; while on the other hand he did not deny the importance of the mental barriers which serve to channel sexuality towards objectives other than its original ones. For this reason he was, and still is, accused of being old-fashioned by those who see the uncontrolled liberation of our instinctual forces as the ultimate aim of self-realization.

Freud's theory advocates neither the liberation of the instincts from all moral and social restraint, nor their repression in order to conform to moral and social reality. This is evident from the way he talks of 'taming' the instincts, a concept which has often been misunderstood:

> 'Is it possible by means of analytic therapy to dispose of a conflict between an instinct and the ego, or of a pathogenic instinctual demand upon the ego, permanently and definitively?' To avoid misunderstanding it is not unnecessary, perhaps, to explain more exactly what is meant by 'permanently disposing of an instinctual demand'. Certainly not 'causing the demand to disappear so that nothing more is ever heard from it again'. This is in general impossible, nor is it at all to be desired. No, we mean something else, something which may be roughly described as a 'taming' of the instinct. That is to say, the instinct is brought completely into the harmony of the ego, becomes accessible to all the influences of the other trends in the ego and no longer seeks to go its independent way to satisfaction. ('Analysis terminable and interminable', standard edn, vol. XXIII, pp. 224—5)

The schools of thought which disagree with Freud on the subject of the impact of society on human behaviour have either come to see adaptation to social reality as the object of their therapy, thus failing to take into account the existence and the nature of the forces of instinct, or they make society responsible for individual neuroses so that it is society which must be transformed in the interests of the freedom of the individual. While the therapist will no doubt have his own views on the subject, and probably he cannot avoid letting one or other attitude colour his therapy to a certain extent, neither has a place in psychological theory.

The *Three Essays on the Theory of Sexuality*, like *The Interpretation of Dreams*, has a far greater scope than the title suggests.

In the first place it is a description of the development of the sexual instinct through the various stages from earliest infancy to puberty.

In this description the concept of sexuality is modified, extended and redefined as a somatic function directed primarily towards pleasure, and only serving the ends of reproduction as a secondary consideration. Even affection and friendship are related to sexuality. The broadening of the concept of sexuality so that it can be understood as being independent of genital sexuality provides a new approach to the problem of sexual deviation. As distinct from merely describing or morally condemning the condition, Freud now seeks to explain how it has developed from an imbalance of partial aims in infancy. It defines the relation between normality and neurosis, between neurosis and perversion.

It lays the foundations for what was to become *analytical characterology*, or the study of character, where character is seen as the habitual way in which we make choices, organize ourselves and defend ourselves against our impulses, all of which we have to do from earliest infancy.

It establishes, tentatively at first, then more boldly, but with constant revision, the still open question of the distinction between 'masculine' and 'feminine' from a psychological point of view.

The Interpretation of Dreams and the *Three Essays on the Theory of Sexuality* form the two base camps of Freud's work for the next 30 years of research, revision, elaboration and constant effort. Even his work which does not deal with clinical research but investigates other fields takes them as starting-points.

10

Other Areas in which Psychoanalysis is Relevant

We have seen how Freud's clinical case histories led him to discover the general relevance of the Oedipus complex, whereupon he turned his attention to works of literature such as Shakespeare's *Hamlet,* and to the ancient myths handed down to us by the great Greek dramatists; and we have noted how in *Totem and Taboo* he studied primitive societies whose tribal taboos are expressed in symbols and customs which are more usually the preserve of anthropologists.

Freud's work on *Totem and Taboo* kindled his interest in the origins of religion and ethics, which were to be discussed many years later in *The Future of an Illusion* (1927) and *Civilization and its Discontents* (1930). With increasing clarity he realized that historical events, the impact human beings make on one another, social evolution and the remaining traces of prehistoric events, of which religion is the principal example, are nothing less than the reflection of the dynamic conflicts between the ego, the id and the super-ego, as studied by the psychoanalyst in the individual, played out on a wider stage.

Once his attention had been drawn to literature as a possible source of illustration for his psychoanalytic theories, Freud analysed various poetic and artistic creations, using the same criteria as for his clinical cases. In his essay *Delusions and Dreams in Jensen's 'Gradiva'* (1907), for instance, Freud interpreted the dreams and reactions of the story's protagonist as if she were an actual patient. He then formulated the hypothesis that the same unconscious mechanisms with which he had become familiar in clinical practice were probably at work in the artistic process. In *Leonardo da Vinci and a Memory of his Childhood,* however, he was interested in both the biographical detail and the creative powers of the artist:

> What psycho-analysis was able to do was to take the inter-relations between the impressions of the artist's life, his chance experiences, and his works, and from them to construct his [mental] constitution and the instinctual impulses at work in it — that is to say, that part of him which he shared with all men. With this aim in view, for instance, I made Leonardo da Vinci the subject of a study, which is based on a single memory of childhood related by him and which aims chiefly at explaining his picture of 'The Madonna and Child with St. Anne'. (*An Autobiographical Study,* standard edn, vol. XX, p. 65)

Psychoanalysis can shed new light on biographical information available to us and can enable us to understand why people choose to behave and express themselves in a particular way. The distinctiveness of Freud's approach to biography lies in the fact that he reverses the connection between actions which are reported as history, and the fantasies, impulses and repressions of the individual's unconscious which cause him to act as he does. In his essay on Leonardo, Freud's analysis of the artist's account of a childhood memory enables him to attempt an interpretation of some of the intriguing aspects of Leonardo's character: his transition from painting to scientific research and back again; his lack of interest in any kind of sexual activity, which led to his being thought entirely asexual; and the creative inhibitions which he suffered in his middle years. Biographical details

viewed from an analytic point of view explain Leonardo's
choice of subject in certain of his pictures: laughing women
and lovely youths in his early years, and in his maturity
women with mysterious enticing smiles, whose expression,
enigmatic and tender, haunted him always.

In other essays Freud concentrated on the creative process
itself. In 'Creative Writers and Day-Dreaming' (1908), for
instance, he asks where the poet, strange creature, gathers his
material, and how he manages to enthrall us with it; and he
compares the activity of the poet, or creative people generally, to the child at play. The technique of the artist is to
manipulate fantasies so as to enable us to enjoy things which
are not normally enjoyable. Since the contents of these
fantasies, like dreams, translate the realization of the artist's
own repressed desires and inclinations, there exists a link
between the artist's work and his own life. Aesthetic pleasure,
like the pleasure we take in games or jokes, results from the
artistic content of the work and in its creation lies the artist's
skill and his particular secret. According to Freud, the
pleasures we gain from the arts enable us to relax the tensions
of the psyche, and in this lies the real reason for our
enjoyment of them.

In answer to the question as to whether psychoanalysis
could reveal the specific secret of artistic creation, Freud
openly admitted that no psychoanalysis can explain Leonardo's
genius. Many years later, in 1924, he wrote: 'The layman may
perhaps expect too much from analysis in this respect, for it
must be admitted that it throws no light on the two problems
which probably interest him the most. It can do nothing
towards elucidating the nature of the artistic gift, nor can it
explain the means by which the artist works — artistic
technique' (*An Autobiographical Study,* standard edn, vol.
XX, p. 65). In essays, private correspondence and in conversations with anyone wishing to discuss contemporary
artistic trends, Freud stated that 'the subject-matter of works

of art has a stronger attraction for me than their formal and technical qualities, though to the artist their value lies first and foremost in these latter' ('The Moses of Michelangelo', standard edn, vol. XIII, p. 211). The point was made by E. H. Gombrich in his collection of essays on *Freud and the Psychology of Art* that in spite of Freud's personal tastes and the views he expressed in certain essays on particular works of art, Freudian theory does provide us with an interpretative tool which enables us to approach the essential secret at the heart of artistic creation. Ernst Kris, a psychoanalyst and pupil of Freud's, wrote in his *Psychoanalytical Explorations in Art* (1962) that Freud's *Jokes and their Relation to the Unconscious* was a model of how the creative process could be analysed along Freudian lines.

In 'Creative Writers and Day-Dreaming' (1908) Freud stresses the similarity already referred to between the creative process and the construction of verbal jokes. This affinity consists in a certain command of means of expression and an interest in the uses to which this can be put, and in a playful enjoyment in amalgamating discordant elements into a whole by a mysterious process. According to Gombrich, Freud's analytical theory enables us to identify the source of this mysterious activity: it is the ego which learns to transmute and analyse the impulses of the id and to unite them in those many-faceted crystals of miraculous complexity which we call works of art. They are the symbols, not the symptoms, of this co-ordinating faculty.

The creative process's affinity with games and jokes lies precisely in its ability to co-ordinate and synthesize fantasies which are the unexpressed and inexpressible potential of real life into meaningful structures through word-play and the play of images. It is this intervention of the ego which distinguishes artistic creation from dreams and from neurotic fantasies. The creative artist also borrows from the world of *primary processes* which is the source of dream distortions and neurotic symptoms. But as Freud points out, 'the artist . . . unlike the neurotic . . . knew how to find a way back from it and once more to get a firm foothold in reality. His creations, works of art . . . differed from the asocial, narcissistic products of dreaming in that they were calculated to arouse sympathetic interest in other people and were able to evoke and to satisfy the same unconscious wishful impulses in them too' (*An Autobiographical Study,* standard edn, vol. XX, pp. 64—5).

It is well known that a cultural movement sprang from Freud's theory which outstripped his own work in this area. This is equally true of his psychoanalytically oriented research in the fields of sociology and politics. As we noted in the second chapter of part I of this study, Freud never focused his attention on a specific political organization. He merely took the view that the collective psyche behaves in a similar way to the individual psyche, and any analysis he made of a collective nature was carried out on this assumption. He based his belief on the fact that during the early stages of socialization in infants, children are permanently influenced by the adults around them who, consciously or not, hand down to them a given social model. In Freud's work the concept of the super-ego, or the child's interiorization of the parental image as authority and law, bridges the gap, as it were, between the psychology of the individual and the psychology of society.

Other psychoanalytically oriented studies have developed what was implicit in Freudian theory: the influence of society on behaviour. H. Heinz Hartmann observed that if one focuses one's attention on the mechanisms of the ego instead of those of the id, psychoanalytical theories can be used to explain the pressure — or even the tyranny — which environmental factors tend to exert on our private inner conflicts. He queries the extent to which a given social structure can bring to the surface, provoke, or reinforce certain instinctual tendencies or certain kinds of sublimation. He believes that research should be carried out into the way various social structures facilitate the solution of certain inner conflicts through participation — real or imagined — in specific social experiences.

Several studies of this nature, in which psychoanalytic methods have been used to give a critical assessment of society, have been carried out, notably by Paul Parin, who has developed theories with implications for the relationship between the analyst and the patient and between the individual and his social environment.

Freud's interests beyond the sphere of clinical psychology paved the way for a mass of studies on ethics, religion, art, folklore and literature, and provoked an interest in psychoanalysis which extended far beyond that in clinical research. His attitude to the value and purpose of these studies was ambivalent. In 'On the History of the Psycho-Analytic Movement' (1914) he stated that his original intention was to see psychoanalysis not as a science which would contribute to other mental sciences, so much as a science which would dominate all others and make people rethink them from within, as it were. Psychoanalysis was not to be 'applied' to other disciplines, or to be allied with them, so much as to be used to renovate them.

In certain passages, however, Freud does seem to consider this aspect of psychoanalysis in a more specific, restricted light. In *An Autobiographical Study* he observes that

> the word 'psychoanalysis' has itself become ambiguous. While it was originally the name of a particular therapeutic method, it has now also become the name of a science — the science of unconscious processes. By itself this science is seldom able to deal with a problem completely, but it seems destined to give important contributory help in a large number of regions of knowledge. The sphere of application of

psychoanalysis extends as far as that of psychology, to which
it forms a complement of the greatest moment. (Standard edn,
vol. XX, p. 70)

Freud himself pointed out the obstacles and risks of error
encountered in his studies in other fields: the scarcity and
arbitrary nature of the biographical data available to the
analyst, an imperfect knowledge of the cultural background
of the time, the fact that analysis itself does not take place in
contact with the patient, but using outside information, thus
lacking the personal contribution of the patient to the process
of interpretation provided by transfer — all these factors
combine to make this sort of investigation a mere 'speculative
hypothesis'.

In *Il vero e il falso* (1979, p. 120), E. Codignola states that,
beyond the sphere of analysis itself, although there is obviously no reason why one should not make use of data
provided by the theory to corroborate hypotheses which
have already been formulated, interpretation in the psychoanalytical sense of the term is not possible. One must
abandon the method, while affirming the general principles
derived from the theory, or make use of psycho-analytical
examples to illustrate facts of a different order (for instance,
of a social, political, or cultural nature). He goes on to say
that it is therefore superfluous to point out the dangers of
such a practice. This does not imply that one should refute
the ability of psychoanalysis to contribute a different view of
anthropology; on the contrary, the method has already
contributed widely to this field; but if one does not respect
the specific nature of its interpretative method it is easy to
trivialize its significance.

Despite these limitations and pitfalls and Freud's own
errors, which his detractors pounced on relentlessly, Freud's
work is still a source of enormous interest because of the
diversity of the subjects he deals with and the way he mixes

clinical data and hypotheses, historical and anthropological knowledge and opinion. His interest in a particular aspect of human activity was never restricted to one specific text, but would crop up again in clinical studies and sociological essays alike, his interests constantly cross-fertilizing one another.

His interest in religion, for instance, a subject to which Freud considered he had contributed more than to any other, stretches from *Totem and Taboo* (1912—13), through *The Future of an Illusion* (1927), to *Moses and Monotheism* (1939). It intermingles with his interest in society in *Totem and Taboo*, *Group Psychology and the Analysis of the Ego* (1921), *Civilization and its Discontents* (1930), and with clinical analyses in 'Obsessive Actions and Religious Practice' (1907).

Similarly, his research into art and literature is linked with clinical analysis and with other activities which, although not pathological, use the language of the unconscious which is defined, because of its particular syntax, as the language of the primary processes. Freud's study of creativity in 'The Relation of the Poet to Day-Dreaming' (1908) refers back to *Jokes and their Relation to the Unconscious* (1905), which in turn refers to *The Psychopathology of Everyday Life* (1901), and they all owe something to *The Interpretation of Dreams* (1900).

Because of the complexity of Freud's work, the way in which, for instance, he would constantly reassess each and every theory and add to its fascinating and far-reaching implications in other fields, it is impossible to summarize Freud's achievement without detracting from its richness.

Here ends my exposition. My aim was to introduce the reader to Freud's philosophy, to retrace his early struggles and demonstrate the peculiarity of his work at its very beginning. Freud's first works contain in embryo the basic premisses on which the vast structure of his philosophy was founded. If I have succeeded in arousing your interest it is now for you to read Freud's own supremely lucid texts and to acquire at first hand an understanding of the author who led the way into unexplored territories of the human mind.

Bibliography

The bibliography includes only those books which have been quoted in the text. The date of the original publication is indicated where this is considered to be significant in the context and is given within parentheses. The dates of the first editions of Freud's works likewise precede the title and are in parentheses.

Ariès, Philippe, *Centuries of Childhood*, London, 1962.

Badinter, Elizabeth, *The Myth of Motherhood*, London, 1981.

Breuer, Joseph (1893–5), *Studies on Hysteria*, Harmondsworth, 1975.

Busch, Wilhelm (1865), *Max und Moritz*.

Codignola, Ernesto, *Il vero e il falso*, Turin, 1979.

Eco, Umberto, 'Il medioevo e già cominciato', in *Documenti sui nuovo medioevo*, Milan, 1973.

Ellenberger, Henri, *The Discovery of the Unconscious*, London, 1970.

Freud, Sigmund (1888–9), Translation with Preface and Notes of H. Bernheim's *De la suggestion et de ses applications à la thérapeutique*, Paris, 1886.

—— (1893), with Breuer, J., *On the Psychical Mechanism of Hysterical Phenomena: Preliminary Communication (Studies on Hysteria*, part I), *The Standard Edition of the Complete Psychological Works of Sigmund Freud*, London, 1953–74.

—— (1895), with Breuer, J., *Studies on Hysteria*, standard edn, vol. II.

—— (1900), *The Interpretation of Dreams*, standard edn, vols IV–V.

—— (1901), *On Dreams,* standard edn, vol. V.

—— (1901), *The Psychopathology of Everyday Life,* standard edn, vol. VI.

—— (1905), *Jokes and their Relation to the Unconscious,* standard edn, vol. VIII.

—— (1905), *Three Essays on the Theory of Sexuality,* standard edn, vol. VII.

—— (1905), 'Fragment of an analysis of a case of hysteria', standard edn, vol. VII.

—— (1907), *Delusions and Dreams in Jensen's 'Gradiva',* standard edn, vol. IX.

—— (1908), 'Character and anal eroticism', standard edn, vol. IX.

—— (1908), ' "Civilized" sexual morality and modern nervous illness', standard edn, vol. IX.

—— (1908), 'Creative writers and day-dreaming', standard edn, vol. IX.

—— (1910), *Leonardo da Vinci and a Memory of his Childhood,* standard edn, vol. XI.

—— (1910), 'The psycho-analytic view of psychogenic disturbance of vision', standard edn, vol. XI.

—— (1910), ' "Wild" psycho-analysis', standard edn, vol. XI.

—— (1912), 'On the universal tendency to debasement in the sphere of love', standard edn, vol. XI.

—— (1912–13), *Totem and Taboo,* standard edn, vol. XIII.

—— (1913), 'An evidential dream', standard edn, vol. XII.

—— (1913), 'On beginning the treatment (further recommendations on the technique of psycho-analysis)', standard edn, vol. XII.

—— (1914), 'The Moses of Michelangelo', standard edn, vol. XIII.

—— (1914), 'On narcissism: an introduction', standard edn, vol. XIV.

—— (1914), 'On the history of the psycho-analytic movement', standard edn, vol. XIV.

—— (1914), 'Remembering, repeating and working-through (further recommendations on the technique of psycho-analysis, II), standard edn, vol. XII.

—— (1915), 'Observations on transference-love (further recommendations on the technique of psycho-analysis, III)', standard edn, vol. XII.

—— (1916—17), *Introductory Lectures on Psycho-Analysis,* standard edn, vols XV—XVI.

—— (1919), 'The "uncanny"', standard edn, vol. XVII.

—— (1921), *Group Psychology and the Analysis of the Ego,* standard edn, vol. XVIII.

—— (1923), *The Ego and the Id,* standard edn, vol. XIX.

—— (1924), 'The dissolution of the Oedipus complex', standard edn, vol. XIX.

—— (1925), *An Autobiographical Study,* standard edn, vol. XX.

—— (1925), 'The resistances to psycho-analysis', standard edn, vol. XIX.

—— (1925), 'Some psychical consequences of the anatomical distinction between the sexes', standard edn, vol. XIX.

—— (1926), *The Question of Lay Analysis,* standard edn, vol. XX.

—— (1927), *The Future of an Illusion,* standard edn, vol. XXI.

—— (1930), *Civilization and its Discontents,* standard edn, vol. XXI.

—— (1931), 'Female sexuality', standard edn, vol. XXI.

—— (1933), *New Introductory Lectures on Psycho-Analysis,* standard edn, vol. XXII.

—— (1937), 'Analysis terminable and interminable', standard edn, vol. XXIII.

—— (1939), *Moses and Monotheism,* standard edn, vol. XXIII.

—— (1950), *The Origins of Psycho-Analysis,* London and New York, 1954. Partly, including 'A project for a scientific psychology', in standard edn, vol. I.

—— (1960), *Letters 1873—1939,* ed. E. L. Freud, trans. T. and J. Stern, New York, 1960; London, 1961.

Hoffmann, E. T. W. (1813—16), *The Devils Elixirs.*

Hofmannsthal, H. von (1893), *Der Tor und der Tod,* trans. in *Poems and Early Plays,* 1961.

Jones, A. Ernest (1953—7), *The Life and Works of Sigmund Freud,* edited and abridged in one volume by L. Trilling and S. Marcus, Harmondsworth, 1964.

Kafka, Franz, 'Letter to his father', in *Wedding Preparations in the Country and Other Posthumous Prose Writings,* London, 1973.

Krafft-Ebing, Richard von (1866), *Psychopathia Sexualis.*

Kris, Ernst, *Psychoanalytic Explorations in Art,* London, 1962.

Kupper, H. and Rollman-Branch, 'Freud and Schnitzler', *American Journal of Psychoanalysis*, 7 (1959), pp. 1098ff.

Laing, Ronald D., *Politics in the Family*, London, 1971.

—— and Esterton, A., *Sanity, Madness and the Family*, London, 1970.

Lasch, C., *The Culture of Narcissism*, New York, 1978.

Lessona, Michele (1928), *Volere e potere*.

Magris, Claudio, *Il mito asburgico nella litteratura austriaca moderna*, Turin, 1976.

Marcuse, H., *Eros and Civilization*, New York, 1955.

Morel, Bénédict-Auguste (1860), *Traité des maladies mentales*.

Musil, Robert, *The Man Without Qualities*, London, 1966.

Parin, Paul, 'L'Io e i meccanismi di adattamento', in *Psicoterapia e scienze umane*, 1—3 (Milan, 1979).

Poe, Edgar Allan (1839—46), *Tales*.

Rapoport, David, *The Collected Papers of David Rapoport*, New York, 1967.

Roazen, Paul, *Freud: società e politica*, Turin, 1973.

Roth, Joseph, *The Radetzky March*, London, 1974.

—— (1927), *Flight Without End*, London, 1977.

—— (1966), *The Silent Prophet*, London, 1979.

Schnitzler, Arthur (1893), *Anatol*.

—— (1919), *Casanova's Homecoming*.

—— (1908), *The Road to the Open*.

Schorske, Carl E., *'Fin de Siècle' Vienna: Politics and Culture*, London, 1979.

Shorter, Edward, *The Making of the Modern Family*, London, 1976.

Stevenson, Robert Louis (1886), *The Strange Case of Dr Jekyll and Mr Hyde*.

Weber, Max, *The Protestant Ethic and the Spirit of Capitalism*, London, 1976.

Wilde, Oscar (1891), *The Picture of Dorian Gray*.

Index